视 频 互 动 版
Video-Text Interactive Version

THE CHINESE STRENGTH

中国中央电视台　中国电影股份有限公司　编著
Compiled by China Central Television and China Film Co., Ltd.

中国画报出版社·北京
China Pictorial Press · Beijing

图书在版编目（CIP）数据

中国力量：汉英对照 / 中国中央电视台，中国电影股份有限公司编著；刘海乐译. -- 北京：中国画报出版社，2019.11
　　ISBN 978-7-5146-1753-5

Ⅰ.①中… Ⅱ.①中…②中…③刘… Ⅲ.①社会主义建设成就 – 中国 – 汉、英 Ⅳ.①D619

中国版本图书馆CIP数据核字(2019)第109453号

中国力量（中英文）
中国中央电视台　中国电影股份有限公司　编著

出 版 人：于九涛
责任编辑：方允仲
执行编辑：朱露茜
特邀审校：张跃平
英文译者：刘海乐
英文定稿：王国振
英文改稿：苏　格（Scott Huntsman）
责任印制：焦　洋

出版发行：中国画报出版社
地　　址：中国北京市海淀区车公庄西路33号　邮编：100048
发 行 部：010-68469781　010-68414683（传真）
总 编 室：010-88417359　版权部：010-88417359

开　　本：12开（889mm×1194mm）
印　　张：17
字　　数：304千字
版　　次：2019年11月第1版　2019年11月第1次印刷
印　　刷：北京汇瑞嘉合文化发展有限公司
书　　号：ISBN 978-7-5146-1753-5
定　　价：260.00元

《中国力量》(中英文)画册 视频互动版
THE CHINESE STRENGTH (VIDEO-TEXT INTERACTIVE EDITION)

Presented by China International Publishing Group
Authorized by China Film Co., Ltd.
Film Planning: Beijing China Film Marketing Co., Ltd.

Book Adapted by China Pictorial Press
Short Video Platform & Technical Support: China Internet Information Center (China.org.cn)
TV Documentary & Film Broadcasting Platform: China Central Television (CCTV, CCTV.com)
Photos Courtesy of: Xinhua News Agency, China News Service, *China Pictorial*, *PLA Daily*, *Guangming Daily*, China.org.cn, China State Railway Group Co., Ltd., China National Offshore Oil Corporation, China Shipbuilding Industry Corporation, Qian Xiaohu, Hou Deqiang, etc.

The Chinese Strength Multilingual Photo Book Editorial Staff
Concept by Lu Cairong
Publisher: Yu Jiutao
Project Coordinator: Fang Yunzhong
Adapted by Fang Yunzhong, Zhu Luxi
Photo Editor: Zhu Luxi
Specially Invited Editor: Zhang Yueping
Chinese Editors: Zhang Yueping, Luo Pingfeng, Liu Xiaoxue
English Editor: Wang Guozhen
English Translator: Liu Haile
English Consultant: Scott Huntsman
English Proofreader: Ye Shujun
Graphic Designer: Zheng Jianjun
Design Director: Zhao Yun (specially invited)
Layout Designers: Zhao Yanchao, Dong Changyi (specially invited)
Video Photo Editor: Zhao Jingmei (specially invited)
Video Editors: Zhao Jingmei, Zhou Mengyuan (specially invited)
Webpage Editors: Dai Fan (specially invited), Song Ruobing (specially invited), Qi Rui (specially invited), Sun Lei (specially invited)

画册出品：中国外文出版发行事业局
版权授权：中国电影股份有限公司
电影策划：北京中影营销有限公司

画册改编：中国画报出版社
短视频平台及技术支持：中国互联网新闻中心（中国网）
电视专题片、电影播放平台支持：中国中央电视台（央视网）
图片提供：新华社、中国新闻社、人民画报社、解放军报社、光明日报社、中国网、中国国家铁路集团有限公司、中国海洋石油集团有限公司、中国船舶重工集团有限公司，钱晓虎、侯德强，等。

《中国力量》多语种画册编创人员
出版策划：陆彩荣
出 品 人：于九涛
项目统筹：方允仲
改　　编：方允仲、朱露茜
配　　图：朱露茜
特邀审校：张跃平
中文审稿：张跃平（特邀）、罗平峰、刘晓雪
英文定稿：王国振
英文译者：刘海乐
英文改稿：苏　格（Scott Huntsman）
英文校对：叶淑君
装帧设计：郑建军
版式指导：赵　云（特邀）
排版设计：赵艳超、董长义（特邀）
视频选图：赵婧梅（特邀）
视频剪辑：赵婧梅、周梦圆（特邀）
网页编辑：戴　凡（特邀）、宋若冰（特邀）、齐　锐（特邀）、孙　磊（特邀）

港珠澳大桥全线亮灯
The Hong Kong-Zhuhai-Macao Bridge is lit up in the evening.

2018年7月1日，"复兴号"动车组从北京南站开出
July 1, 2018: A Fuxing bullet train departs from the Beijing South Railway Station.

京新高速公路
The Beijing-Xinjiang Expressway.

2019年10月1日，庆祝中华人民共和国成立70周年大会在北京天安门广场隆重举行。图为受阅空中梯队从北京上空飞过

October 1, 2019: A military parade in honor of the 70th anniversary of the founding of the People's Republic of China is held at Tian'anmen Square in Beijing. Pictured is an air echelon flying over Tian'anmen Square.

2016年10月17日，"神舟十一号"载人飞船在甘肃省酒泉卫星发射中心成功发射
October 17, 2016: The Shenzhou-11 manned spacecraft is successfully launched at the Jiuquan Satellite Launch Center in Gansu Province.

2010年11月12日，"天宫一号"空间实验室与神舟飞船进行空间交会对接的电脑模拟图
A photomontage shows the Shenzhou spacecraft docking with the Tiangong-1 space lab in space on November 12, 2010.

扫码看同内容电影
Scan to watch the film

前言
FOREWORD

时光如水，日月如梭。但那些伟大的历史瞬间，总是会被人们铭记。

2017年10月18日，在中国共产党第十九次全国代表大会上，中共中央总书记、国家主席习近平说："十八大以来的五年，是党和国家发展进程中极不平凡的五年。""五年来的成就是全方位的、开创性的，五年来的变革是深层次的、根本性的。""经过长期努力，中国特色社会主义进入了新时代，这是我国发展新的历史方位。"

这是砥砺奋进的五年，这是真抓实干的五年，这也是取得历史性成就的五年。

进入新时代的这五年，中国国内生产总值年均增速在世界主要经济体中位居第一，中国对世界经济的贡献率超过30%，成为拉动全球经济的第一引擎。

中国人民有了更多的获得感、幸福感、安全感。

创新、协调、绿色、开放、共享的新发展理念正赋予中国全新的发展动能。

中华民族伟大复兴的宏伟誓愿，正在世界的东方回响。

同心同德，同向同行。

美好生活，正在每一个中国人手中创造。

Time marches on, but many fleeting historical moments may be remembered forever.

On October 18, 2017, Chinese President Xi Jinping, also general secretary of the Communist Party of China (CPC) Central Committee, declared at the 19th CPC National Congress: "The five years since the 18th National Congress have been a truly remarkable five years in the course of the development of the Party and the country." "The achievements of the past five years have touched every area and broken new ground; the changes in China over the past five years have been profound and fundamental." "With decades of hard work, socialism with Chinese characteristics has crossed the threshold into a new era. This is a new historic juncture in China's development."

These five years brought historic achievements earned through painstaking efforts and concrete action.

During these five years, China bested all major economies in the world in terms of GDP growth rate and contributed more than 30% of global economic growth, becoming the core engine driving the world economy.

With this, Chinese people have a strong sense of fulfillment, happiness and security.

In this period, China pursued with firmness the vision of innovative, coordinated, green, and open development that is for everyone.

The Chinese dream of national rejuvenation is being realized.

Chinese people are working hard with one mind and an enterprising spirit.

扫码看同内容电影
Scan to watch the film

目录 CONTENTS

前言
FOREWORD

001-037 第一章 圆梦工程
Ⅰ REALIZATION OF CHINESE DREAM

038-067 第二章 创新驱动
Ⅱ INNOVATION-DRIVEN DEVELOPMENT

068-091 第三章 协调发展
Ⅲ COORDINATED DEVELOPMENT

092-117 第四章 绿色中国
Ⅳ A GREENER CHINA

118-139 第五章 共享小康
Ⅴ SHARED PROSPERITY

140-155 第六章 开放中国
Ⅵ A MORE OPEN CHINA

156-183 第七章 共筑中国梦
Ⅶ BUILD THE CHINESE DREAM TOGETHER

后记
POSTSCRIPT

视频目录　VIDEOS' CONTENTS

前言
FOREWORD

第一章　圆梦工程
I　REALIZATION OF CHINESE DREAM

003　中国桥
CHINESE BRIDGES

015　中国路
CHINESE ROADS

017　中国车
CHINESE VEHICLES

023　中国港
CHINESE PORTS

029　南水北调
THE SOUTH-TO-NORTH WATER DIVERSION PROJECT

033　天然气管网
THE GAS PIPELINE NETWORK

035　特高压工程
ULTRA-HIGH VOLTAGE PROJECTS

037　中国网
CHINA'S TELECOM NETWORK

第二章　创新驱动
II　INNOVATION-DRIVEN DEVELOPMENT

041　中国大飞机
CHINA'S LARGE AIRCRAFT

043　水陆两用飞机
CHINA'S AMPHIBIOUS AIRCRAFT

045　大型运输机
CHINA'S LARGE MILITARY CARGO JET

047　海上钻井平台
CHINA'S OFFSHORE DRILLING PLATFORMS

051　载人深潜器"蛟龙号"
CHINA'S DEEP-SEA MANNED SUBMERSIBLE "JIAOLONG"

053　中国天眼
CHINA'S "HEAVENLY EYE"

059　载人航天工程
CHINA'S MANNED SPACE PROGRAM

060　探月工程
CHINA'S LUNAR EXPLORATION PROGRAM

061　量子研究
QUANTUM RESEARCH

063　"天宫二号"空间站
CHINA'S SPACE LAB TIANGONG-2

067　充满活力的创新力量
VIGOROUS INNOVATION

第三章　协调发展
III　COORDINATED DEVELOPMENT

071　西藏扶贫
POVERTY ALLEVIATION IN TIBET

075　精准扶贫
TARGETED POVERTY ALLEVIATION

077　"闽宁模式"
THE "FUJIAN-NINGXIA COOPERATION MODEL"

081　木渎镇
MUDU TOWN

087　设立雄安新区
THE ESTABLISHMENT OF XIONG'AN NEW AREA

089　四大板块协调发展
COORDINATED DEVELOPMENT OF THE FOUR REGIONS

第四章 绿色中国
IV A GREENER CHINA

095 建设自然保护区
THE ESTABLISHMENT OF NATURE RESERVES

105 修复海洋生态
MARINE ECOLOGICAL RESTORATION

109 发展绿色能源
THE DEVELOPMENT OF GREEN ENERGY

113 绿水青山就是金山银山
LUCID WATERS AND LUSH MOUNTAINS ARE INVALUABLE ASSETS

第五章 共享小康
V SHARED PROSPERITY

121 振兴教育
THE REVITALIZATION OF EDUCATION

125 繁荣文化
THE PROSPERITY OF CULTURE

131 病有所医
MEDICAL SERVICES ARE ACCESSIBLE TO ALL

135 老有所养
THE ELDERLY WILL BE LOOKED AFTER PROPERLY

137 安全保障
SECURITY ASSURANCE

第六章 开放中国
VI A MORE OPEN CHINA

143 也门撤侨
THE EVACUATION OF OVERSEAS CHINESE IN YEMEN

145 中欧班列
CHINA-EUROPE FREIGHT TRAINS

147 "一带一路"倡议
THE BELT AND ROAD INITIATIVE

153 国际会议上的中国声音
CHINA'S VOICE AT INTERNATIONAL CONFERENCES

第七章 共筑中国梦
VII BUILD THE CHINESE DREAM TOGETHER

159 大美山河
BEAUTIFUL LANDSCAPES

163 城市更加繁荣
PROSPEROUS CITIES

167 社会事业蓬勃发展
VIGOROUS DEVELOPMENT IN ALL ASPECTS OF SOCIETY

169 国防和军队建设
MILITARY DEVELOPMENT AND NATIONAL SECURITY

175 全面对外开放
FULLY OPENING UP

177 民族团结，共同实现中国梦
ALL ETHNIC GROUPS UNITE TO REALIZE THE CHINESE DREAM

扫码看同内容电影
Scan to watch the film

扫码看同类专题片
Scan to watch similar documentaries

第一章

▶ 圆梦工程
I REALIZATION OF CHINESE DREAM

在最鲜活的生活中，人们触摸到五年来一个个圆梦工程给中国社会带来的改变，这些变化坚强、有力、迅猛而又温暖地铸就着这个国家前行的每一个脚印。

中国桥、中国路、中国车、中国港、中国网……

成就十三亿多人民福祉的中国梦，已触手可及。

驱动中国复兴的创新引擎，正全速前进。

Chinese people are already feeling the tremendous changes in daily life and Chinese society brought by projects carried out to fulfill the Chinese Dream. Those changes have robustly and profoundly reinforced every step of the nation along the road forward while warming hearts.

Chinese bridges, roads, vehicles, ports, networks....

Every new connection brings over 1.3 billion Chinese closer to the realization of the Chinese Dream of national rejuvenation.

Driving an engine of innovation, China is rolling forward at full speed.

CHINESE BRIDGES

Numerous bridges in China are reshaping the country's economic and geographic reach.

The Hong Kong-Zhuhai-Macao Bridge finally reached closure over the waters of the Lingdingyang Sea. Zhenhua 30, the world's largest crane ship, was independently designed and built by China. The colossal vessel, 297 meters long and 58 meters wide and with displacement of nearly 250,000 tons, is bigger than any aircraft carrier in service in the world.

It immediately headed for the waters of the Lingdingyang Sea, where it performed placement of the final closure joint of the Hong Kong-Zhuhai-Macao Bridge.

May 2, 2017: Lin Ming, chief engineer of the Hong Kong-Zhuhai-Macao Bridge, at the construction site of the project.

"When I joined the project 12 years ago, I was 48 years old," notes Lin Ming, chief engineer of the Hong Kong-Zhuhai-Macao Bridge project. "Today as the final closure joint of the bridge is installed, I'm 60 years old. Over the decade we worked on this project, our nation has witnessed rapid progress and realized dreamlike development. I seized the world's best equipment, engineering methods and techniques, which ensured that the bridge was the best project in the globe."

On May 2, 2017, he final closure joint of the Hong Kong-Zhuhai-Macao Bridge begins installation, while Lin Ming serves as the site engineering commander.

"In 1992, when the Zhuhai Bridge—also a cross-sea bridge—installed its final closure joint, the largest engineering vessel we found available throughout the Pearl River estuary was only a 500-ton ship," recalls Lin Ming. "Today, we used a 12,000-ton vessel to complete the final closure of the Hong Kong-Zhuhai-Macao Bridge. The gigantic ship is the world's largest full-swing crane vessel, and it was independently built by China. Its water displacement and size are equivalent to two or three aircraft carriers. It is mind-blowing."

Workers hang suspension cables weighing a total of four tons onto the final closure joint. Each cable measures 120 meters in length and 40 centimeters in diameter and is made of 140,000 high-intensity fibrils. They can support objects as heavy as 12,000 tons and rotate 360 degrees.

"Never before has anyone in the world rotated a tunnel joint weighing more than 6,000 tons in the air like we did," adds Lin Ming.

Over the past four years, Lin and his coworkers successfully installed 33 immersed tubes, all of which only needed to be connected once. But this final tube needed to be connected on both sides simultaneously. The adjustment allowance for installing this undersea tube was only a dozen centimeters. Even when the surface of the sea was calm and placid, underwater currents could still generate heavy thrusting forces.

To ensure the closure joint was precisely installed in the preset mounting slot, the crane vessel Zhenhua 30 had to maintain absolute stability on the sea.

"China has undergone significant changes after decades of reform and opening up," declares Lin Ming. "If you compare our past projects, equipment and designs with today's Hong Kong-Zhuhai-Macao Bridge, you have to conclude that our nation can achieve anything it wants."

Lin Ming commands the construction site, and he says: "Zhenhua 30, drop E1 by four centimeters."

中国桥

一座座中国桥,重塑着中国经济地理的新标志。

伶仃洋海面,港珠澳大桥最终接头工地。"振华30",这艘世界上最大的起重船,完全由中国自主制造。这个长度超过二百九十七米,宽度五十八米,排水量接近二十五万吨的庞然大物,体量超过了世界上所有现役航空母舰。

它正前往伶仃洋海域,完成一项世界瞩目的工程——港珠澳大桥最终接头安装。

扫码看本节短视频
Scan to watch the short video

❀ 鸟瞰港珠澳大桥
A bird's-eye view of the Hong Kong-Zhuhai-Macao Bridge.

港珠澳大桥总工程师林鸣说:"十二年前参与这个工程的时候,我四十八岁。今天进行最终接头的安装,我已经满六十岁了。在我们做这个工程的时候,国家确实突飞猛进,像梦一样地发展,在这里看到的,是全球最好的装备、最好的工法、最好的工艺、也是最好的工程。"

2017年5月2日,林鸣担任港珠澳大桥现场工程指挥,最终接头的合龙安装正式开始。

林鸣说:"1992年,珠海大桥也是在海中间,当时找遍珠江口,最大的一条船五百吨。截止到今天,到2号(最终接头日)那天,是用一个一万二千吨的,一个全球最大的全回转的(船),我们自己制造的,排水量是航母的两三倍,大航母的两三倍,这样一个东西。你想,才几天啊,别的行业我相信也不会差。"

工人们把四吨重的吊带挂在最终接头上。每根吊带长一百二十米,直径四十厘米,由十四万根高强度纤维丝组成,它的臂力最多能吊起一万二千吨重物并做三百六十度回旋。

"全世界没有人把一根六千多吨的东西去这么转一下,没有一个人敢在我们之前去转过。"

林鸣他们过去四年已经成功安装了三十三根沉

港珠澳大桥局部图
A shot of the Hong Kong-Zhuhai-Macao Bridge.

作业中的"振华30"大型起重船
The Zhenhua 30 crane ship in operation.

"振华30"大型起重船
The Zhenhua 30 crane ship.

珠澳口岸人工岛，"振华30"大型起重船参与港珠澳大桥施工
The Zhenhua 30 crane ship works at the construction site of the Zhuhai-Macao frontier port island of the Hong Kong-Zhuhai-Macao Bridge.

"Copy that! E1 dropping four centimeters." The woker at the installation site replies.

The worker says: "There are still 40 centimeters for E1 to sink in the mounting slot."

"Before this project, the national standard of error tolerance for suspending cables was 2%, which meant that 100 meters allowed an error of two meters and 60 meters an error of 1.2 meters," said Lin Ming. "We managed to shrink the error tolerance to 1.5 centimeters. In fact, it doesn't make a difference for this project whether the error is one millimeter or 10 centimeters. But if you can shrink the error to one millimeter through tenacious efforts, it is more than eliminating tiny errors—it demonstrates the nation's engineering capacity. This is crucially important."

"If all industries and sectors work together to achieve such a goal, our nation will become unprecedentedly strong," he adds.

建成后的港珠澳大桥全景
A panoramic view of the Hong Kong-Zhuhai-Macao Bridge.

管,但都只需要单侧对接。而这根最终接头,不仅要完成双侧对接,而且水下安装余量仅有十几厘米。即使水面风平浪静,海底涌动的洋流也会形成巨大的推力。最终接头能否精准嵌入安装基槽,需要"振华30"保持绝对平稳。

林鸣说:"我们国家已经改革开放发展这么多年,你过去看工程,看(到)的是有什么装备,(就)设计什么样的方案。你今天看我们港珠澳工程,你要得到这样一个结论,只要你想怎么干,我们国家现在都有能力制造一些专门的东西,能够干成。"

林鸣现场指挥:"'振华30',一号落四公分(即厘米)。"

现场工人回复:"好的,一号落四公分。"

现场工人说:"距离着床还有四十公分,还有四十公分。"

林鸣说:"吊带在我们这个工程之前国家标准是2%,一百米差两米,六十米的话就是差一点二米,我们要把它解决掉一点五公分的这个问题。一个毫米跟十公分对这个工程是一样的,是一回事,但你要能做一个毫米的时候,通过你的努力,你控制(着)能做成一个毫米,它反映的就不是一个毫米的问题,也可以说是你的一个国力——国家力量,这样一个展示,它的意义极为重大。"

"各行各业如果都去实现一个梦的时候,这个国家将会变得无比强大。"

港珠澳大桥桥体近景
Part of the Hong Kong-Zhuhai-Macao Bridge.

地处港珠澳大桥珠澳口岸人工岛的珠海公路口岸夜景
The Zhuhai Railway Port, which is located on the Zhuhai-Macao frontier port island of the Hong Kong-Zhuhai-Macao Bridge, at dusk.

中国力量 THE CHINESE STRENGTH

CROSS-SEA BRIDGES

"A bridge connects two sides of a natural moat." One after another bridges in China have become legends of the country's engineering prowess and milestones of the development of national strength.

2009年12月25日,浙江舟山跨海大桥建成通车,它是目前世界上规模最大的岛陆联络工程
The Zhoushan Cross-Sea Bridge in Zhejiang Province, which opened to traffic on December 25, 2009, is the world's largest island-mainland connection project.

2013年5月28日,厦漳跨海大桥通车运营
The Xiamen-Zhangzhou Cross-sea Bridge, which began operation on May 28, 2013.

青岛胶州湾跨海大桥,于2011年6月30日通车运营
The Qingdao-Jiaozhou Bay Bridge, which opened to traffic on June 30, 2011.

跨海大桥

"一桥飞驾南北,天堑变通途。"中国桥,正书写着中国工程一个又一个传奇,也持续刷新着中国国力的一座又一座里程碑。

◎ 杭州湾跨海大桥连接嘉兴市和宁波市,采用恶劣条件下的海上长大桥梁建造技术,于2008年5月1日通车运营
The Hangzhou Bay Bridge, which began operation on May 1, 2008, links Jiaxing and Ningbo cities. The project involves many advanced sea-crossing bridge engineering technologies to overcome harsh conditions.

CROSS-RIVER BRIDGES

In addition to cross-sea bridges, many river bridges in China have consecutively set world records. More than 100 bridges have been built or are still under construction over the Yangtze River.

Bridges in the mountainous areas in west China link many formerly secluded remote places to the outside world, facilitating circulation of the country's economic arteries.

武汉天兴洲长江大桥，于 2009 年 12 月 26 日通车运营，是目前世界上最大的公铁两用桥
The Wuhan Tianxingzhou Yangtze River Bridge, which opened to traffic on December 26, 2009, is the largest highway-railway bridge in the world.

武汉长江大桥是中华人民共和国成立后修建的第一座公铁两用长江大桥
The Wuhan Yangtze River Bridge is the first highway-railway bridge over the Yangtze River built after the founding of the People's Republic of China in 1949.

南京大胜关长江大桥，建成时是全球第一座六线铁路大桥，是世界上跨度最大的高速铁路桥，也是世界上设计荷载最大的高速铁路桥
The Dashengguan Bridge in Nanjing is the world's first six-track railway bridge. It is also the high-speed railway bridge with the largest span and the fastest designed speed in the world.

跨江大桥

除跨海大桥之外，同样在刷新世界纪录的还有中国的跨江大桥。今天仅在长江上已建好和在建的桥梁就突破了一百座。

西部大山里的中国桥打通了曾经的偏远断点，它们让中国的经济血脉变得更加畅通。

◎ 鹦鹉洲长江大桥
The Yingwuzhou Yangtze River Bridge.

位于云贵交界的北盘江第一桥，于2016年12月29日竣工运营，是世界第一高桥
The Beipan River Bridge, located on the border of Yunnan and Guizhou provinces and completed on December 29, 2016, is the world's highest bridge.

中国力量 THE CHINESE STRENGTH

CHINESE ROADS

Countless highroads comprise a transport network that enhances China's economic efficiency. The county boasts an expressway network with a total length of 131,000 kilometers, ranking first in the world. It is estimated that the total length of China's expressways will reach 150,000 kilometers by 2020.

⊛ 鹤大高速是自东北东部出海往朝鲜、韩国、日本等东北亚地区开展国际贸易的快捷通道
The Hegang-Dalian Expressway provides a convenient conduit for goods from northeastern China to reach the coast and then be exported to Northeast Asian countries such as the Democratic People's Republic of Korea (DPRK), the Republic of Korea, and Japan.

⊛ 青藏铁路连接着青海省西宁市和西藏自治区拉萨市,是通往西藏腹地的第一条铁路,也是世界上海拔最高、线路最长的高原铁路
The Qinghai-Tibet Railway linking Xining City of Qinghai Province with Lhasa City of the Tibet Autonomous Region is the first railway towards the backland of Tibet and the world's longest plateau railroad with the highest altitude.

中国路

扫码看本节短视频
Scan to watch the short video

一条条中国路，勾勒出中国经济高效运行的新版图。十三万一千公里的中国高速公路网，总里程世界第一。2020年，中国高速公路将达到十五万公里。

❂ 川藏公路北线，雀儿山隧道贯通。雀儿山海拔5050米，曾经山鹰都飞不过的山峰，现在车辆十分钟就能翻越
Completion of the Que'er Shan Tunnel along the north line of the Sichuan-Tibet Highway enables drivers to pass through the 5,050-meter-high mountain that even blocks eagles in just 10 minutes.

❂ 京新高速是连接北京和乌鲁木齐的高速公路，是世界上穿越沙漠戈壁最长的高速公路，于2019年4月23日基本全线贯通
The Beijing-Xinjiang Expressway, completed on April 23, 2019, provides the longest stretch of road across a desert landscape in the world.

CHINESE VEHICLES

High-speed trains have become new engines driving China's economic development.

China's high-speed rails are considered symbolic of Chinese achievements in the new era.

"复兴号"动车生产车间，工人们正在工作。2012年中国标准动车组"复兴号"正式启动研发
Workers at a Fuxing train assembly workshop. China officially launched the project to develop Fuxing EMU trains in 2012.

A bullet train Fuxing rolls off the assembly line on June 25, 2017 for the first time.

A standard EMU (Electric Multiple Units) train is built in three steps: carriage, bogie and assembly.

A total of 14,000 laborers work on three production lines. Each train consists of more than 550,000 components in 7,100 categories, and workers maintain zero error in assembly.

"As early as 2013 when the EMU project was first launched, we had already set the goal of 100% independent design and manufacturing, including train carriages and all related components," says Fu Shanqiang, telecommunication system engineer for the Fuxing train project. "Both hardware and software were independently designed and completed by Chinese people."

Of the 254 key standards that the Fuxing high-speed train meets, 84% were formulated by China.

As the "heart" of the Fuxing train, each traction convertor features 1,152 IGBT chips that enable a high-speed train to operate smoothly. This technology was monopolized by a few manufacturing powers for more than three decades until China made breakthrough in 2014.

中国车

扫码看本节短视频
Scan to watch the short video

让中国奔跑起来的还有中国车,它们正在给经济换上新引擎。

中国车,已成为中国"创时代"的新标志。

组装中的"复兴号"动车
Fuxing EMU trains in an assembly workshop.

2017年6月25日,"复兴号"下线。

这是中国第一列标准动车组"复兴号"。

一列标准动车的组装,分为车体、转向架、总装三部分。

三条生产线上,一万四千名工人,要安装列车上七千一百多种、总计五十五万多个零部件,他们能做到零差错。

"复兴号"动车组电信系统工程师付善强说:"我们整个标准动车组在2013年论证的时候就已经明确提出了要自主化,包括整车,包括所有的关联系统、零部件、软件、硬件,都要全部实现自主化。全都是由中国人自己独立完成。"

"复兴号"涉及的高速动车组二百五十四项重要标准中,中国标准占到了84%。

一台牵引变流器有一千一百五十二个IGBT芯片,是"复兴号"的心脏。三十多年来,这种能让高铁平稳运行的芯片一直被少数制造强国垄断。2014年,中国在这方面的技术取得了突破。

眼前这条IGBT生产线,每年能制造十二万个芯片。它们不止用于高铁,还用于智能电网、航空航天、新能源等领域。

中国高铁的研发,至少拉动着三十万家零部件

The IGBT production line is capable of manufacturing 120,000 chips each year which are widely used in high-speed rails as well as other sectors like intelligent power grids, aerospace and new energy.

China's high-speed industry has injected impetus into the development of at least 300,000 relevant components and parts manufacturers.

Every core breakthrough in the development of Chinese standards has led to an improvement of the entire industrial system.

Chinese President Xi Jinping called high-speed trains a "beautiful calling card" of China's equipment manufacturing sector during his inspection tour to CRRC Changchun Railway Vehicle Co., Ltd. on July 17, 2015.

The Fuxing bullet train, which is now used in China, runs at a speed as fast as 350 kilometers per hour, cutting the travel time from Beijing to Shanghai to 4.5 hours.

Today, China rivals any competitors in terms of high-speed rail technology including traditional high-speed rail powers such as Japan and Germany.

Taking a train on one of the beautiful railways creates a picturesque painting of China's development as it unfolds before the passenger's eyes when the train passes prosperous metropolises and the vast and vibrant countryside. So far, the total length of high-speed railways in China has reached 25,000 kilometers, more than the combined length of the nine countries ranking second to tenth, of which nearly 60% were constructed in the past five years.

It is projected that a high-speed railroad network comprised of eight longitudinal and eight latitudinal lines, with a total length of 45,000 kilometers, will take shape in China by 2030, becoming a new source of pride for the nation.

一列标准动车的组装，分为车体、转向架、总装三部分
A standard EMU train is built in three steps: carriage, bogie and assembly.

蓄势待发的"复兴号"动车
Fuxing bullet trains in a rail yard.

企业的发展。

中国标准的意义,就在于每一项核心突破,拉动的都是整个体系的升级。

2015年7月17日,习近平主席考察中国中车长春轨道客车时说:"高铁,中国产的动车,这个是中国的一张亮丽的名片。"

投入运营的"复兴号"时速高达三百五十公里,从北京到上海只要四个半小时。

与日本、德国等高铁强国相比,今天中国在高铁技术领域已不逊色于任何一位竞争对手。

登上最美铁路,领略大美风光,车轮滚动出一幅崭新的中国画卷。穿越繁华都市,纵横田野阡陌。二万五千公里的中国高铁,总里程超过第二至第十位国家的总和,其中近六成都是这五年建成的。

2030年,一个八纵八横,总规模约四万五千公里的高速铁路网将彰显中国铁路建设的新骄傲。

❀ 海南环岛高铁,是列车与大海的美丽邂逅
The Hainan ring high-speed railway allows passengers to enjoy picturesque seascapes.

❀ 兰新高铁,尽览雪山草场映衬下的西部风情
The Lanzhou-Xinjiang high-speed railway enables passengers to enjoy the magnificent scenery of the western wilderness including snow-capped mountains and boundless grasslands.

❀ 哈大高铁,中国最北端的"极地特快"
The Harbin-Dalian high-speed railway is dubbed the "Polar Express" in the northernmost corner of China.

❀ 京津高铁,成就三十分钟城市圈
The Beijing-Tianjin intercity rail cuts the travel time between the two cities to about 30 minutes.

中国力量 THE CHINESE STRENGTH

2006年7月1日,青藏铁路全线开通
The Qinghai-Tibet Railway, which was completed and began operation on July 1, 2006.

CHINESE PORTS

As a major global trader, China contributes nearly one-fourth of the total trade volume of the planet.

Increasingly growing cargo throughput requires China to accelerate harbor construction. Of the world's 10 largest ports in terms of throughput, seven are in China.

China is also home to the world's largest port machinery manufacturing base. More than 80% of mechanical equipment operating in ports along the coastlines worldwide was made in China.

China ranks first in the world in volume of shipbuilding orders and quantity of ships built and delivered. The country is capable of building 95% of all types of vessels in the world.

内河第一大港苏州港，江海河联运让这里的内河吞吐量增速位列全球之首
The port of Suzhou, the largest inland river harbor in China, has become the fastest-growing river harbor in the world in terms of throughput thanks to the development of river-sea combined transportation.

The Phase IV of the Shanghai Yangshan Port, the largest in the world, has begun operation. Featuring automated cranes and logistics vehicles, operation of the terminal is controlled by only nine human workers. The terminal, equipped with 10 quay cranes, 30 rail-mounted gantry cranes, wharfs and stockyards, resembles a massive chessboard. There, 130 automated guided vehicles can sense its position with the help of the 61,199 magnetic markers on the ground and chooses the most optimal route according to the need of loading tasks and real-time traffic conditions.

The intelligent terminal increases work efficiency by 30%. It takes 10 hours less than before to load or unload one of the world's largest container carriers at the terminal.

Currently, the Shanghai Port, where Yangshan Port is located, has an annual throughput of more than 40 million TEUs. The port is just one window on China's opening to the world. Of the world's 10 largest ports in terms of throughput, seven are in China.

On the southern coast of China, three international deep-water ports—Guangzhou, Shenzhen and Hong

中国港

扫码看本节短视频
Scan to watch the short video

作为世界贸易大国，这个星球上有近四分之一的贸易额在中国产生。

持续增长的吞吐量，要求中国的港口必须再提速。全球吞吐量排名前十的超级大港，中国已经包揽了七席。

世界上最大的港机制造基地也在中国。纵览全球海岸线，超过80%的港机都是中国制造。

中国的船舶订单量、建造量和未交付订单占有率三大指标均为世界第一。世界上已有船只类型95%以上中国人都能造。

❂ 宁波舟山港，2016年刷新吞吐量纪录，成为全球第一个九亿吨大港
In 2016, Zhoushan Port in Ningbo set a world record by achieving throughput surpassing 900 million tons.

全球第一大港——上海洋山港四期码头已投入运营。装卸现场，只见吊车和自动导引运输车忙碌，却空无一人。这里的生产控制只需要九个人。十台岸桥，三十台轨道吊，码头和堆场就像一个巨大的棋盘。一百三十辆自动导引运输车会根据地下埋藏的六万一千一百九十九根磁钉，感知自己的位置，同时按照实时装载需要和路况，选择最经济的路线。

智能码头作业效率可以提升30%，意味着目前世界上最大的集装箱船在这里装卸能比以前节省十个小时。

如今洋山港所在的上海港，年吞吐量已突破四千万标准箱。这仅仅是中国融通全球的枢纽之一。全球吞吐量排名前十的超级大港，中国已经包揽了七席。

海岸线的南端，广州、深圳与香港三个国际深水良港紧紧相连。它们手挽着手，为珠三角数以百万计的工厂助力，让世界爱上中国造。

但中国的工程师并未就此满足。世界上最大的港机制造基地也在中国。纵览全球海岸线，超过80%的港机都是中国制造。

中国的船舶订单量、建造量和未交付订单占有率三大指标均为世界第一。世界上已有船只类型95%以上中国人都能造。

巨轮远航，向海而生。从海洋回望内陆，纵横跨越中国版图的一个个超级工程，正在绘制中国资源调度的鸿篇巨制。

广州、深圳、香港三港联运为珠三角数以百万计的工厂助力
The combined transport service provided by Guangzhou, Shenzhen and Hong Kong ports boosts the development of millions of factories in the Pearl River Delta.

上海洋山深水港，截至 2018 年，是全球最大的智能集装箱码头
The Yangshan deep-water port in Shanghai remained the world's largest container terminal by 2018.

Kong—work hand in hand to distribute China-made products from millions of factories in the Pearl River Delta region to the world.

However, Chinese engineers and builders expect such ports to play an even greater role in the future. China is also home to the world's largest port machinery manufacturing base. More than 80% of mechanical equipment operating in ports along the coastlines worldwide was made in China.

China ranks first in the world in volume of shipbuilding orders and quantity of ships built and delivered. The country is capable of building 95% of all types of vessels in the world.

China resembles a huge ship sailing across the ocean. From sea to inland, one by one, "super projects" are carried out throughout the country's vast territory, optimizing China's resource allocation to historic levels.

❀ 航行中的中国制造的船舶（组图）
Chinese-made vessels on voyage.

广州、深圳、香港三港联运之香港
The port of Hong Kong has cooperated with Guangzhou and Shenzhen ports to provide joint transport services.

THE SOUTH-TO-NORTH WATER DIVERSION PROJECT

Known as the world's largest water conservancy program, the South-to-North Water Diversion Project has transported water equal to 770 West Lakes in Hangzhou, benefiting more than 100 million people in China. As a result, exploitation of underground water in northern China has reduced by 800 million cubic meters. The underground water level in Beijing rises for the first time in 16 years.

⊛ 航拍"南水北调中线工程"渠首大坝
An aerial view of a dam of the South-to-North Water Diversion Project.

⊛ 南水北调工程大坝周围山清水秀（组图）
The picturesque landscapes of a reservoir of the South-to-North Water Diversion Project.

南水北调

扫码看本节短视频
Scan to watch the short video

南水北调，这个世界上最大的水利工程，从南到北搬运了七百七十个西湖，已有超过一亿人受益，地下水开采因此减少八亿立方米。北京地下水十六年来首次出现了回升。

❀ 南水北调工程缓解了我国北方地区水资源短缺的问题
The South-to-North Water Diversion Project helps relieve water shortage of northern China.

❀ 南水北调工程输水渠
A canal of the South-to-North Water Diversion Project.

南水北调中线丹江口水利枢纽大坝
The Danjiangkou Dam in the middle route of the South-to-North Water Diversion Project.

THE GAS PIPELINE NETWORK

The second pipeline of the West-to-East Gas Transmission Project has begun full operation. With a total length of nearly 20,000 kilometers, the gas pipeline network covers 17 Chinese provinces, municipalities and autonomous regions as well as the Hong Kong Special Administrative Region. It enables 400 million Chinese people to access clean energy.

西气东输二线鸟瞰图，西气东输工程能够促进我国能源结构和产业结构调整，带动东部、中部、西部地区经济共同发展
A bird's-eye view of the second pipeline of the West-to-East Gas Transmission Project. The gas transmission project is conducive to improving China's energy structure and industrial structure and promoting common development of the eastern, central and western regions of the country.

天然气管网

扫码看本节短视频
Scan to watch the short video

西气东输二线已经全线投产，近两万公里的天然气管网覆盖全国十七个省区市和香港特别行政区，四亿中国百姓用上了清洁能源。

◎ 西气东输管道铺设
The West-to-East Gas Transmission Project under construction.

◎ 西气东输二线管道检查作业
The second pipeline of the West-to-East Gas Transmission Project under inspection.

ULTRA-HIGH VOLTAGE PROJECTS

Workers install a 1,000-kV ultra-high voltage power transmission project, which is connected to a large clean energy base about 1,000 kilometers away in western China. Over the past five years, China has completed 12 world-class ultra-high voltage projects, and another eight are still under construction.

不惧危险，在高空开展一千千伏特高压工程高空作业的工人
A worker installs wires for a 1,000-kV ultra-high voltage power transmission project in the air.

特高压能大幅提升我国电网的输送能力
Through the use of ultra-high voltage technology, China's power grid has greatly enhanced its electricity transmission capacity.

架设在群山峻岭间的特高压线
Ultra-high voltage transmission lines running through mountains.

特高压工程

凌空走钢丝的工人们，正在建设的一千千伏特高压工程，连接着上千公里外的西部大型清洁能源基地……仅这五年，中国投入运营的世界级特高压工程就有十二个，还有八个正在建设。

❀ 一千千伏特高压工程高空作业场景
Workers install 1,000-kV ultra-high voltage transmission lines.

❀ 一条条特高压线为中国大江南北带来清洁能源
Ultra-high voltage transmission lines bring clean energy to almost every corner of China.

❀ 在"钢丝"上作业的工人
Electricity workers on power transmission lines.

❀ 特高压工程高空远景
Ultra-high voltage transmission lines viewed from distance.

扫码看本节短视频
Scan to watch the short video

CHINA'S TELECOM NETWORK

Information resources have become an increasingly important productive factor and sector of social wealth since the turn of the 21st Century. In this context, China introduced the internet power strategy. So far, the country has built the world's largest 4G network with 2.99 million base stations and 890 million users. It has installed optical fibre cables totaling 30.41 million kilometers, of which 60% were deployed in the past five years.

在高空作业的工作人员
A worker on duty.

检查通信相关设备
Checking equipment.

中国网

扫码看本节短视频
Scan to watch the short video

进入二十一世纪，信息资源日益成为重要的生产要素和社会财富，中国提出了网络强国战略。二百九十九万个基站，八点九亿用户，中国已经建成全球规模最大的4G网络，光缆线路总长已达三千零四十一万公里，其中有60%都是这五年铺设的。

◎ 中国已经建成全球规模最大的4G网络
China has established the world's largest 4G network.

◎ 中国4G网络飞速发展
China's 4G network has seen rapid development.

◎ 中国4G网络基站
A 4G base station on the mountaintop.

扫码看同内容电影
Scan to watch the film

扫码看同类专题片
Scan to watch similar documentaries

第二章

▶ 创新驱动
II INNOVATION-DRIVEN DEVELOPMENT

锐意创新、敢为人先，中国创新的沃土上，新一代正全面接棒。创新驱动发展，一个创新型的国家，正越来越近。

With an enterprising and innovative spirit, Chinese people are now taking the lead in many fields. The new generation has accepted the baton of innovation. Owing to its innovation-driven development policy, China is increasingly closer to becoming a major innovative country.

CHINA'S LARGE AIRCRAFT

During his visit to the manufacturing base of China's large passenger aircraft C919 in Shanghai on May 23, 2014, Chinese President Xi Jinping remarked that as the world's largest airplane market, China spends hundreds of billions of yuan purchasing aircraft. He stressed that we should get past the mindset that purchasing is preferable to manufacturing and renting is even better than purchasing. Instead, he urged the country to invest more money in research and development of our own large aircraft to foster capacity in independent manufacturing.

On May 5, 2017, the Chinese dream of building a large aircraft eventually came true.

According to Zhou Guirong, deputy chief designer of the C919, breakthroughs made when developing the C919 are more important than the product itself–they have enabled China to build up its R&D system and capacity for large aircraft.

The integrated avionic system is the "nervous system" of the aircraft. The movement of pulling the yoke, which looks simple, generates and transmits some 10 million transmission signals per second and requires over 1,000 devices to react correspondingly. Previously, only Boeing and Airbus had developed integrated avionic systems for large aircraft, and they fiercely guarded relevant technologies

展翅高飞——C919大飞机飞向蓝天
China's first homemade large passenger aircraft, the C919, makes a test flight.

航电系统是飞机的神经系统
Avionic system is the "nervous system" of an aircraft.

C919大型客机副总设计师周贵荣
Zhou Guirong, deputy chief designer of the C919.

中国大飞机

扫码看本节短视频
Scan to watch the short video

2014年5月23日，习近平主席考察C919制造基地时说，我们这个国家也是最大的飞机市场，每年的话要成百上千亿的都花在这个买飞机上，过去那个逻辑是造不如买、买不如租，我们现在要花更多的钱来研制，制造自己的飞机，形成我们独立的自主的这种能力。

2017年5月5日，中国人百年的大飞机梦，迎来了梦想成真的一刻。

C919大型客机副总设计师周贵荣说："我们这个本身研制成功的突破，不仅仅是研制一个产品，而是把我们整个研发的体系、我们的能力给建立起来了。"

航电系统，飞机的神经系统。这上面整流板如果要配合的话，看似简单的拉杆动作，每秒会产生上千万个传输信号，需要一千多个设备配合工作。此前，全球只有波音、空客拥有大飞机航电系统的集成能力，并且对相关技术严密封锁。

2017年5月5日，C919在上海首飞成功
May 5, 2017: China's first homemade large passenger aircraft, the C919, completes its maiden flight in Shanghai.

研制、安装中的C919大飞机
The C919 in the assembly workshop.

逐渐成型的C919大飞机
The C919 is gradually taking shape in the assembly workshop.

CHINA'S AMPHIBIOUS AIRCRAFT

Now the C919 isn't the only large aircraft made by China.

China's AG600, the world's largest amphibious aircraft designed for fighting forest fires and performing marine rescue missions, rolled off the assembly line in 2016, filling a void in large emergency rescue equipment.

An AG600 amphibious aircraft rolls off the assembly line.

An AG600 amphibious aircraft in the workshop.

水陆两用飞机

中国的大飞机，不止 C919。

世界上最大的水陆两用飞机 AG600 于 2016 年顺利下线，填补了中国大型应急救援装备的空白。

扫码看本节短视频
Scan to watch the short video

✪ 我国自主研制的目前世界上最大的水陆两用飞机 AG600
China's AG600 is known as the world's largest amphibious aircraft.

CHINA'S LARGE MILITARY CARGO JET

China's first domestically built large military cargo jet, the Y-20, made its successful maiden flight in 2013 and has been commissioned by the Chinese Air Force in 2016, ranking China among only a few countries capable of independently designing and developing large aircraft over 200 tons.

"运－20"起飞
China's first domestically built large military cargo jet, the Y-20, takes off from the airport.

"运－20"降落时举行的喷水仪式
A water-splashing ceremony to celebrate the landing of the Y-20.

大型运输机

扫码看本节短视频
Scan to watch the short video

"运-20"于2013年首飞成功,并且于2016年正式列装空军,实现了中国大型运输机零的突破。中国成为世界上少数几个能自主研制二百吨级大型机的国家之一。

✱ "运-20"在空中飞行
The Y-20 flying in the air

✱ "运-20"雄姿(组图)
The Y-20 in the air.

CHINA'S OFFSHORE DRILLING PLATFORMS

Offshore drilling platforms are called "moving national territories" and demonstrate a country's overall industrial strength. Just a few years ago, China was unable to independently build oil platforms on the sea. Today, however, it can build world-class drilling platforms on its own.

"Blue Whale II", the world's largest drilling rig, conducted tests for propeller installation in 2018 in Yantai, Shandong Province. The drilling platform is equipped with eight propellers, which enable it to withstand Force 15 hurricanes.

The "Blue Whale I" oil rig returned from its expedition to the South China Sea, creating a world record by ceaselessly and safely drilling flammable ice for 60 days. And then China's homemade oil platform "Blue Whale II" successfully sailed its maiden voyage in 2018.

The gigantic "Blue Whale II" drilling platform rises as high as a 37-story building and features a deck as big as a football field. It is designed to operate on the sea with a depth of over 3,000 meters and can drill as deep as 15,240 meters, the deepest in the world. It is also the world's largest offshore oil rig.

"蓝鲸一号"俯拍图
An aerial view of the "Blue Whale I" oil rig.

海上钻井平台

扫码看本节短视频
Scan to watch the short video

　　海上钻井平台被称为"流动的国土",是一个国家整体工业实力的重要体现。几年前,中国还完全没有自主制造海上钻井平台的能力。现在,不仅能够自己建造,而且领先全球。

　　山东烟台,全球最大的海上钻井平台"蓝鲸二号"正在进行推进器的安装检查。这样的推进器一共有八个,它的存在足以帮助"蓝鲸二号"在十五级飓风下屹立不动。

　　"蓝鲸一号"此前刚刚出征南海,创造了可燃冰安全开采六十天的世界纪录。而"蓝鲸二号"于2018年实现了首航。这个海上"巨无霸",有三十七层楼高,甲板有一个足球场大。它可以在水深超过三千米的海域作业,最大钻井深度一万五千二百四十米。这是全球最大,钻井深度最深的海上钻井平台。

"蓝鲸二号"首航
China's homemade oil platform "Blue Whale II" sails its maiden voyage.

中国力量 THE CHINESE STRENGTH

◎ 海上"巨无霸""蓝鲸一号"
The magnificent "Blue Whale I" oil rig.

中国力量 THE CHINESE STRENGTH

CHINA'S DEEP-SEA MANNED SUBMERSIBLE "JIAOLONG"

China has implemented a strategy of becoming a maritime power by optimally utilizing its oceanic resources. To this end, it has developed many world-leading deep-water submersibles to explore the ocean.

China's deep-sea manned submersible "Jiaolong" has completed 152 experimental dives. More and more mysteries in the deep sea have been discovered.

China's deep-sea submersible reaches a depth of 11,000 meters in the Mariana Trench, the deepest point in the ocean globally.

Tremendous changes have taken place in the country's maritime exploration.

载人深潜器"蛟龙号"即将进行深海作业
China's manned submersible "Jiaolong" is ready for deep-sea scientific exploration mission.

"蛟龙号"入水瞬间
China's manned submersible "Jiaolong" dives into the water.

"蛟龙号"在海水里下沉
China's manned submersible "Jiaolong" dives deep into the sea.

载人深潜器"蛟龙号"

扫码看本节短视频
Scan to watch the short video

依海富国,以海强国,建设海洋强国,一个个世界领先的深水重器接连入水。

深海载人深潜器"蛟龙号"已经完成一百五十二次试验性应用下潜,地质领域、生物领域……越来越多的海底奥秘被发现。

地球最深处——马里亚纳海沟,也有了中国深潜器的身影,深海一万一千米,这是中国人标记的未来。

节物风光不相待,桑田碧海须臾改。

❂ 作为"蛟龙号"载人深潜器专用母船,"深海一号"是我国首艘按照绿色化、信息化、模块化、便捷化、舒适化和国际化原则设计建造的国际先进水平的全球级特种调查船
As the dedicated mother ship for the manned submersible "Jiaolong", the Shenhai-1 is the first globally advanced research vessel built by China in line with the principles of ecologically-friendliness, informationization, modularization, convenience, comfortableness and internationalization.

❂ "蛟龙号"在深海中潜行
The manned submersible "Jiaolong" explores in the deep sea.

❂ "蛟龙号"在深海抓取样本
The manned submersible "Jiaolong" grabs samples from the seabed.

中国力量 THE CHINESE STRENGTH

CHINA'S "HEAVENLY EYE"

Whether a country can develop into a major power with global influence depends on its strength in basic science.

The largest radio telescope in human history, China's Five-hundred-meter Aperture Spherical Radio Telescope (FAST) is 10 times as sensitive as the famous Arecibo Radio Telescope. From a bold dream to a reality, construction of FAST lasted 22 years across three generations of scientists and engineers and their tireless efforts. Dubbed "Heavenly Eye" in China, FAST consists of 4,450 adjustable reflecting panels, supported by a huge web woven with more than 7,000 steel cables.

Completion of FAST will provide mankind an unblocked view of deep space.

FAST 射电望远镜的最终选址
The location of FAST, the largest radio telescope in the world.

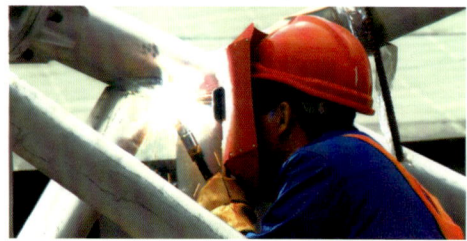
工人在 FAST 射电望远镜施工现场作业
A worker at the construction site of FAST.

FAST 射电望远镜施工现场
The construction site of FAST.

Nan Rendong (1945-2017), chief engineer and scientist of the FAST project, during a media interview. This was his last interview before his death. According to Nan Rendong, the Dawodang depression, where FAST is located, was selected from more than 300 candidates.

In fact, FAST is a space laboratory in extreme physical conditions. The most challenging coming task for the astronomers is to use this facility to create scientific outcomes to serve the nation and the public.

If the FAST radio telescope were an eye, the feed cabin would be its pupil. Suspended by six steel cables, the 30-ton feed cabin hangs precisely in the air, with error of less than 10 millimeters. Such accuracy was unprecedented in world engineering history.

By December 2017, the FAST had discovered nine Pulsars.

中国天眼

扫码看本节短视频
Scan to watch the short video

一个国家能否成为有世界影响力的大国，需要基础科学领域的响亮发声。

FAST是人类历史上最大的射电望远镜，综合性能是著名望远镜阿雷西博的十倍。从一个大胆的设想到最终实现，FAST跨越二十二年，历经三代科技工作者前赴后继，为之奋斗一生。七千多根钢缆织起的这张巨网，是世界上跨度最大、精度最高的索网工程。四千四百五十块反射面板，每一块都可以转动。

中国天眼的发明意味着人类观测太空已不存在任何死角。

FAST射电望远镜总工程师兼首席科学家南仁东（1945—2017）生前最后一次接受采访时说："我们的FAST台址——大窝凼洼坑是我们从三百多个候选洼地里边挑选出来的。"

"它实际提供了一个极端物理条件下的太空实验室。它下一步最艰巨的任务，就是怎么使（用）好这个科学的利器，使它有产出，回馈国家，回馈公众。"

如果说FAST是眼睛，馈源舱就是它的瞳孔。用六根钢索拉起馈源舱，将重达三十吨的舱体，在高空精准定位，误差不超过十毫米，这样的工程难度世界上前所未有。

到2017年12月，FAST已经发现九颗脉冲星。

七千多根钢缆构成这一世界上跨度最大、精度最高的索网工程
FAST is supported by a huge web woven with more than 7,000 steel cables, the largest of its kind in the world.

FAST射电望远镜反射面板安装
Workers install reflecting panels for FAST.

2016年9月25日,位于贵州省黔南州平塘县克度镇大窝凼群山之中的FAST工程落成启用
September 25, 2016: FAST, a radio telescope located in mountains of Pingtang County, Guizhou Province, is put into operation.

中国力量 THE CHINESE STRENGTH

● FAST 射电望远镜全貌
An aerial view of FAST.

中国力量 THE CHINESE STRENGTH

CHINA'S MANNED SPACE PROGRAM

Advancement of science and technology fuels the prosperity of a nation. A country's power derives from its strength in science and technology.

Chinese scientists are working hard to fulfill the nation's dream of space exploration.

Chinese President Xi Jinping spoke with astronauts in the Shenzhou-11 spacecraft at the command center of China's manned space program in Beijing, November 9, 2016.

Xi ensured the astronauts who lived in space for more than half a month that all people across the nation cared for their safety.

The astronauts asserted that they were proud of their mother country.

The average age of the research staff for China's space program is about 30 years old, younger than their counterparts globally.

Young scientists in important positions have become a potential advantage for China's technological innovation.

2015年7月25日，我国在西昌卫星发射中心用"长征三号乙"运载火箭及"远征一号"上面级，以"一箭双星"方式成功发射两颗新一代北斗导航卫星
July 25, 2015: A Long March 3B carrier rocket blast off from the Xichang Satellite Launch Center, sending two BeiDou Navigation Satellites into space.

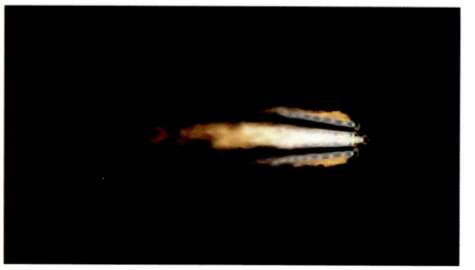

火箭发射夜景
A rocket launched at night.

执行"神舟十一号"载人飞行任务的航天员景海鹏（左）和陈冬
Jing Haipeng (left) and Chen Dong, both astronauts participating in the Shenzhou-11 manned spaceflight mission.

载人航天工程

扫码看本节短视频
Scan to watch the short video

科技兴，则民族兴。科技强，则民族强。

中国的科学家们正在苍穹间为中国筑梦。

2016年11月9日，在中国载人航天工程指挥中心，习近平主席同"神舟十一号"航天员通话。

习近平主席说，你们已经在太空生活了半个多月，全国人民都很关心你们。

航天员说，我们为伟大祖国感到骄傲和自豪。

中国航天一线科研人员平均只有三十多岁，这是让全世界航天人都羡慕的年龄。

年轻人挑大梁，正成为中国创新的隐形利器。

载人航天火箭发射架
A launch pad for manned spacecraft.

2018年11月1日23时57分，中国在西昌卫星发射中心用"长征三号乙"运载火箭，成功发射第四十一颗北斗导航卫星
A Long March 3B carrier rocket to be launched at the Xichang Satellite Launch Center. At 11:57 p.m. on November 1, 2018, the rocket blasted off and sent the 41st BeiDou Navigation Satellite into space.

中国力量 THE CHINESE STRENGTH

探月工程
CHINA'S LUNAR EXPLORATION PROGRAM

扫码看本节短视频
Scan to watch the short video

2013 年 12 月 14 日，"嫦娥三号"月球探测器首次实现月球软着陆。自软着陆以来，"嫦娥三号"创造了在月工作时间全球最长的纪录。

China's lunar probe Chang'e-3 has completed a soft landing on the Moon on December 14, 2013. Since then, it set a world record for the longest work time for an active lunar probe.

2013 年 12 月 14 日，"嫦娥三号"月球探测器成功软着陆于月球雨海西北部
December 14, 2013: China's lunar probe Chang'e-3 achieves a soft landing in the northwestern part of Mare Imbrium on the moon.

自月面软着陆以来，"嫦娥三号"月球探测器创造了全世界在月工作最长纪录，于 2016 年 8 月 4 日正式退役
China's lunar probe Chang'e-3 set a world record as the longest working man-made probe on the moon. It stopped operating on August 4, 2016.

量子研究
QUANTUM RESEARCH

2017年8月10日,世界首颗量子卫星"墨子号"提前实现全部既定科学目标,中国量子通信领跑世界。

On August 10, 2017, the world's first quantum satellite, Micius, has achieved all preset goals ahead of schedule, marking China taking the lead globally in the field of quantum communications.

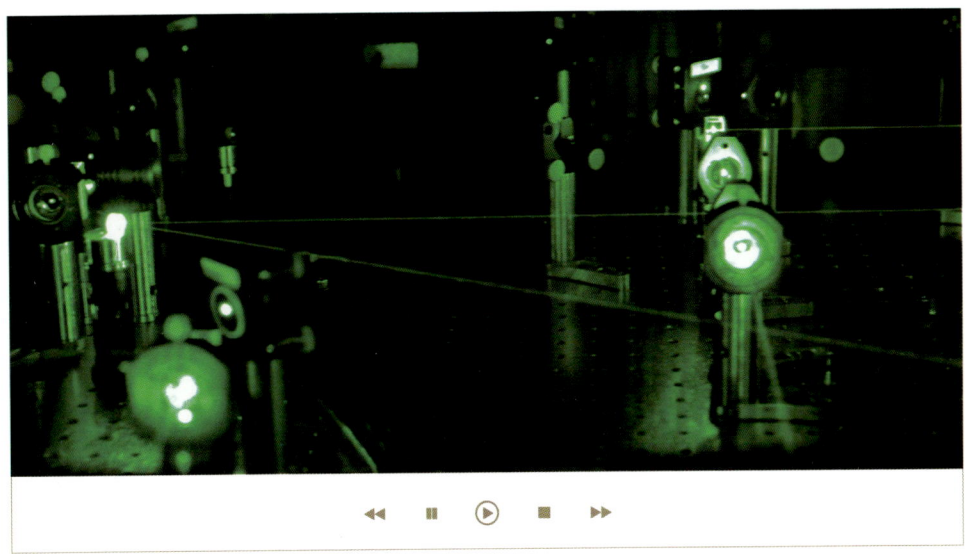

❀ 中国量子研究处于世界最前沿
China takes the lead globally in the field of quantum communications.

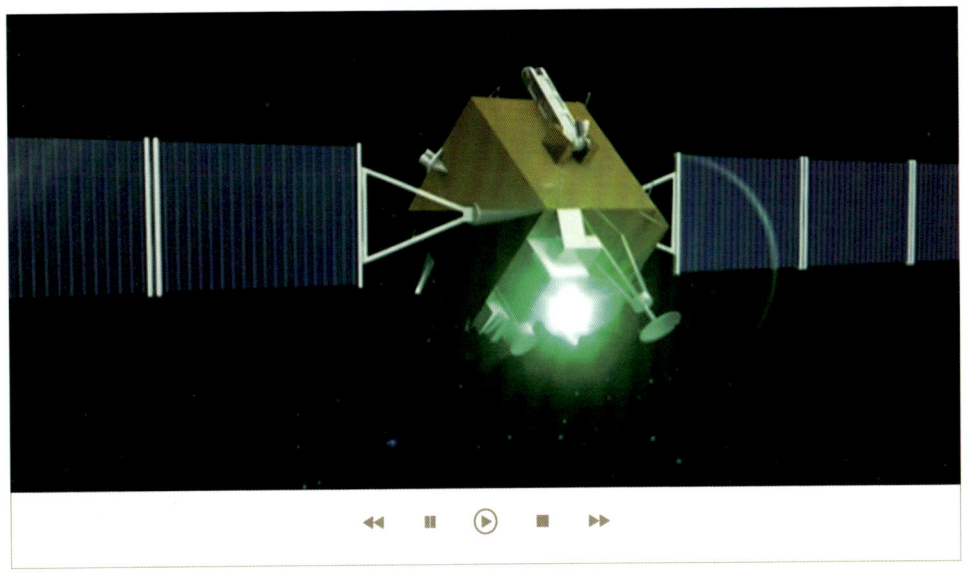

❀ 世界首颗量子卫星"墨子号"
Micius, the world's first quantum satellite.

CHINA'S SPACE LAB TIANGONG-2

The Tiangong-2 is China's first space lab in the true sense. International space experts predict China to be the only country to operate a space station by the year 2024, when the current International Space Station is decommissioned.

September 15, 2016: A Long March FT2 rocket carrying the Tiangong-2 space lab is launched at the Jiuquan Satellite Launch Center in Gansu Province.

"天宫二号"空间站

扫码看本节短视频
Scan to watch the short video

"天宫二号",这是中国第一个真正意义上的空间实验室。国际航天专家预测,2024年中国将成为世界上唯一拥有空间站的国家。

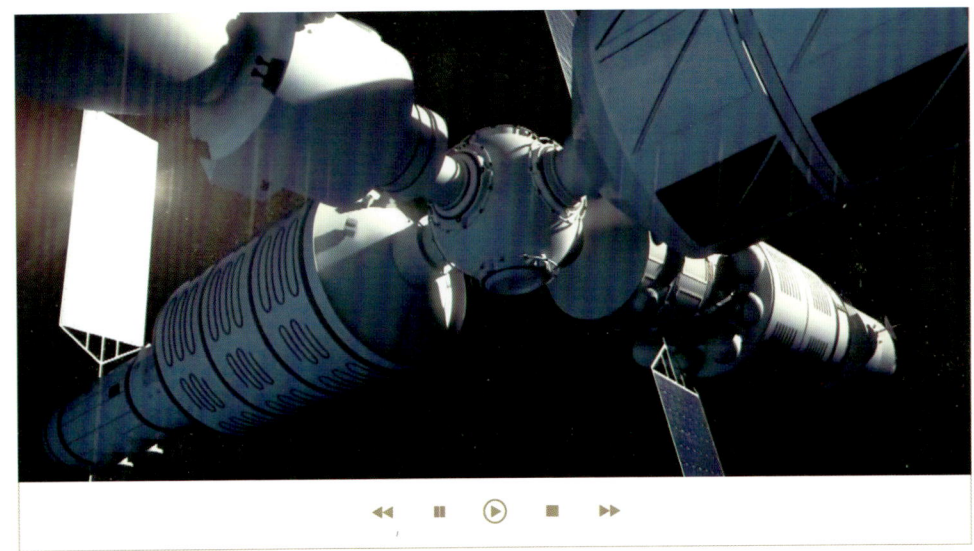

✵ "天宫二号"空间站局部图
China's Tiangong-2 space lab.

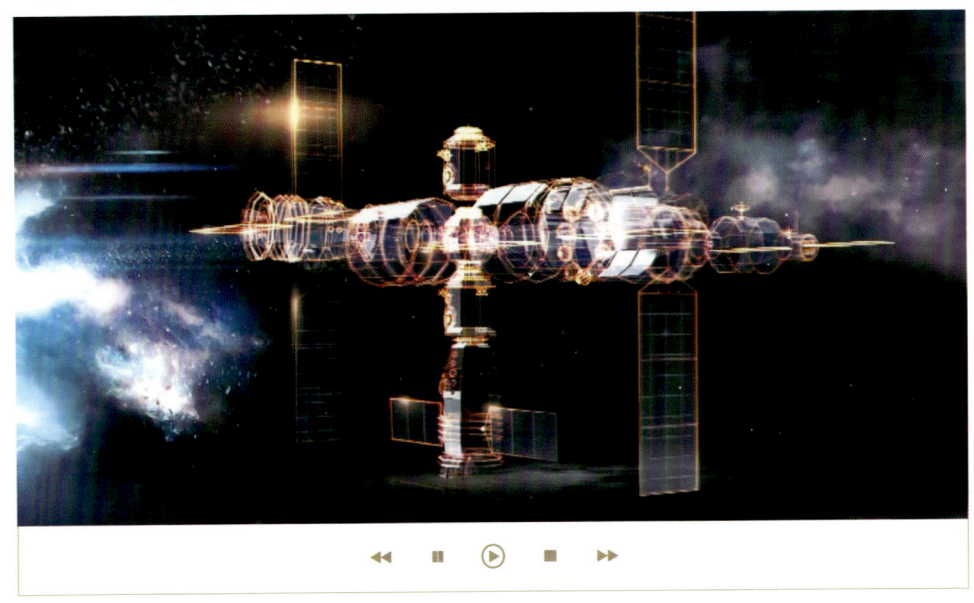

✵ "天宫二号"空间站整体图
A panoramic view of China's Tiangong-2 space lab.

中国力量 THE CHINESE STRENGTH

2016年10月19日,"神舟十一号"与"天宫二号"实现自动交会对接
October 19, 2016: The Shenzhou-11 spacecraft automatically docks with the Tiangong-2 space lab.

VIGOROUS INNOVATION

Chinese President Xi Jinping visited the Institute of Advanced Technology at the University of Science and Technology of China, April 26, 2016. Xi noted that as China opens up further to the world, hundreds of thousands of Chinese students go abroad to study each year, and that many homegrown talent and overseas returnees join in research programs in China. Now, China needs to cultivate and utilize human capital from around the world while training its own talent.

The future belongs to the young generation. Fostering plentiful young innovators is key to activating the country's innovation vigor and kindling hope for scientific and technological progress.

成都，充满活力的年轻人将引领超导磁悬浮列车的未来
The research team comprised of vigorous young people in Chengdu, capital of Sichuan Province, is determining the future of China's superconducting maglev vehicle.

合肥，平均年龄只有三十五岁的量子科学团队，接连实现了量子通信、量子计算的重大突破，中国已站在全球量子研究的最前沿
The quantum research team in Hefei, Anhui Province, at an average age of 35, has consecutively completed major breakthroughs in quantum communications and quantum computing, securing China's position at the top globally in terms of quantum research and development.

充满活力的创新力量

2016年4月26日,中国科技大学先进技术研究院。习近平主席说,现在这么开放,来去自由,我们每年的留学生就是几十万,有很多我们土生土长的,也有很多海归,现在的话,择天下之英才而育之、而用之,我们自己是可以培育出我们的人才。

未来总是属于年轻人的。拥有一大批创新型青年人才,是国家创新活力之所在,也是科技发展希望之所在。

❀ 西安,平均年龄三十出头的飞机研发团队被国际同行誉为最年轻的设计大脑
The research team in Xi'an, Shaanxi Province, at an average age of about 30, is dubbed the "youngest brain" of aircraft development by their international counterparts.

❀ 无锡,国家重点实验室里,年轻人的双手刚刚创造出全球晶硅太阳能电池效率的世界纪录
In the national key laboratory in Wuxi, Jiangsu Province, young researchers have created a world record for high-performance crystalline silicon solar cells.

扫码看同内容电影
Scan to watch the film

扫码看同类专题片
Scan to watch similar documentaries

第三章

▶ 协调发展
Ⅲ COORDINATED DEVELOPMENT

经历了数十年的高速发展之后,近年来中国的人均国内生产总值已经跃上八千美元大关,但新的主要矛盾也应运而生。

2017年10月18日,习近平总书记在中国共产党第十九次全国代表大会上说,中国特色社会主义进入新时代,我国社会主要矛盾已经转化为人民日益增长的美好生活需要和不平衡不充分的发展之间的矛盾。

中国正在直面贫富差距、城乡差距、区域差距三大挑战。

历史正记录下那些携手共进的共同跨越。

After decades of rapid development, China's per-capita GDP exceeds US$8,000. At the same time, the principal contradiction in Chinese society has changed.

On October 18, 2017, General Secretary and Chinese President Xi Jinping said at the 19th CPC National Congress that as socialism with Chinese characteristics has entered a new era, the principal contradiction facing Chinese society has evolved. What we now face is the contradiction between unbalanced and inadequate development and the people's ever-growing needs for a better life.

Today, China is facing three major challenges: wealth inequality, imbalance of rural and urban development and an economic gap between regions.

However, through measures aimed at coordinated development, different regions and groups in China are achieving common prosperity.

POVERTY ALLEVIATION IN TIBET
THE ROLE OF THE "FIRST SECRETARY"

China intends to eradicate poverty by 2020. This would require lifting 20 people out of poverty per minute. Poverty alleviation is a battle in which every second counts. To achieve this goal, a total of 775,000 village officials are working hard in the country's rural areas.

A total of 195,000 first village Party secretaries and 775,000 officials have been dispatched to China's poverty-stricken rural villages to help eradicate poverty there, a move that shows the Chinese government's determination to win the great battle against poverty.

"I began to work with the village committee in June 2015," said Lodra, first secretary of the Trashigang Village Party Committee in Dagze County, southwestern China's Tibet Autonomous Region. "My main job has since been poverty relief."

According to Lodra, grassroots poverty alleviation workers are extremely important, and any bit of carelessness could result in severe consequences. "I hope every statistical number I recorded is accurate," she said.

"After a policy is formulated, it must be disseminated through meetings, but more importantly implemented in practice so it is known to everyone. Moreover, different impoverished households need tailored policies. Each impoverished household might require a unique solution to shake off poverty. This is an arduous task to be sure."

Lodra went to village Ladroma's home and told her some state subsidy policies for children's education. "Your family has a kid at college, so you get a higher living allowance," Lodra told Ladroma. "In the past, the allowance for your family was 200 yuan per month, and it rises to 600 yuan per month now."

"The living allowance helps my family a lot," Ladroma said emotionally. "Thank the Communist Party of China! Long live the Communist Party of China!"

For Lodra, the biggest concern was how to lift Losang Tendar's family out of poverty. The local township government believed that relocation was the best way to help the family shake off poverty.

According to Lodra, at first he didn't want to leave his home village. One reason was he worried about his farmland. He made a living by farming almost his entire life and felt empty after retiring from growing crops and seeing his farmland left idle.

"The solution was to rent out his farmland so he could earn some rental income and set his heart at ease," said Lodra. "I can't remember how many times I visited Losang to urge him to move over the past couple of years. My visits were so frequent that he started getting a bit reluctant to see me," Lodra admitted.

This is Lodra's second visit to Losang Tendar in a week. This time she brought someone interested in renting Losang's farmland. Lodra spent a long time to find this potential renter.

However, Losang refused to sign the relocation agreement once again.

Although unmarried, 25-year-old Lodra often feels like a mother. She worries about almost everything concerning the poverty-ridden households. "I worry so much that sometimes my good intentions are misunderstood," said Lodra. "When they finally seize a much better life, they will understand what I am doing now."

Lodra accompanied Losang to his new home. More than 200 impoverished households from six towns in Dagze County have moved here. The new village built for them was beyond Losang Tendar's imagination, and he was eager to find out how life would be there.

西藏扶贫
进村入户的第一书记

扫码看本节短视频
Scan to watch the short video

2020年，中国要彻底消除贫困，意味着平均每分钟要脱贫约二十人，这确实是一场分秒必争的决战。为了这个目标，全国有七十七万五千名驻村干部在奔忙。

十九万五千名第一书记驻村，七十七万五千名干部帮扶，这是中国在消除贫困这场伟大斗争中的决心。

西藏自治区拉萨市达孜县扎西岗村第一书记洛措说："我是2015年6月份开始在这个扎西岗村委会（工作的），干了两年，主要工作就是做扶贫。"

洛措说，基层工作人员是最重要的，一点都不敢马虎，因为我希望我统计的每一个数字都是最准确的。

"政策不仅仅是上传下达，开个会，宣传一遍就完了。做到位，做到人人都知道，就是因户施策，就是每一户有每一户的方案。（要做到）每一户有每一户的办法，是很难很难的。"

洛措来到村民拉卓玛家，向她讲述小孩上学的一些国家补贴政策。洛措说："家里不是有上大学的小孩吗？生活补贴上有一些变化，以前每个月是200元，现在每个月是600元。"

拉卓玛说："小孩的生活补贴对我家庭很有帮助，感谢共产党，中国共产党万岁。"

洛措最放心不下的，就是罗桑旦达一家。根据乡里的评估，最适合罗桑家的脱贫办法就是易地搬迁。

洛措说："他可能最大的担忧有两点吧，一是他自己的土地放在这边（空着）。他种了一辈子地，有时候他就说，我走了这块田空着，就没人种，（那）就不好。他可能不种田自己心里也会觉得空落落的，（应该是）那种感觉吧。想办法找个租户把他的农田租出去，他自己可以拿点租金，可能土地上面，他就放心了。就这两年做他的工作，我也都记不清楚去找了他多少次了。今天找了他一趟，明天再去找他一趟，人家就可能有点不愿意见我。"

这是洛措这周第二次来罗桑家，今天她带来了愿意承包罗桑家土地的租户，这个租户也是她联系了好长时间才找到的。

可这一次，罗桑还是不愿意签。

西藏自治区拉萨市达孜县扎西岗村第一书记洛措
Lodra, first secretary of the CPC Trashigang Village Committee in Dagze County, Tibet Autonomous Region.

扎西岗村第一书记洛措（右）与村民拉卓玛
Lodra (right) talking with villager Ladroma.

◎ 安置点附近整齐的工业园区
An industrial park near the resettlement village.

Losang Tendar, is satisfied with his new home. "The house is gorgeous," he said.

Less than one kilometer from the new village are an agro-industrial park, a brewery and a handicraft industrial park. Losang Tendar's daughter may seek employment after they move in.

All relocation points are complete with industries that can help new immigrants earn a living. So far, about 10 million impoverished people like Losang Tendar have been relocated.

For Tibetans, the tenth day of each month on the Tibetan calendar is a time to pray for blessings.

Colorful prayer flags dance in the breeze, conveying people's warm wishes for future.

Lodra, first secretary of Trashigang Village Party Committee in the Tibet Autonomous Region, hopes locals seize happy and rich lives.

洛措说:"我觉得自己(好像没结婚)都当妈妈了,我才二十五岁。因为他们自己不操心的事情,我常常需要替他们操心。他(们)也不理解你的苦心。想到他们将来可能过上幸福的生活,就想到这儿的时候,我想他们将来肯定能懂我的那种心情。"

洛措还是想再试一次,一大早她就带着罗桑来安置点。达孜县六个乡镇的两百多户贫困人家已经搬到了这里。新家的环境超出了罗桑旦达的想象,他不停地打听着这里的生活。

在安置点,罗桑旦达对新家很满意,他说:"好得很,漂亮得很。现在看到了就高兴极了,房子质量好,什么都好,感谢政府。"

距离安置点不到一公里就有农业产业园、酿酒厂,还有制作手工艺品的工业园区。罗桑大爷的女儿,将来可以在这里上班。

搬得出、稳得住,所有安置点都有配套产业。像罗桑家一样,全国已经有一千万贫困人口进行了易地搬迁。

藏历初十,祈福的日子。随风起舞的五彩经幡,寄托着大家美好的愿望。

洛措说:"我希望他们将来过上衣食无忧的日子,希望他们的生活越来越美好,越来越富裕,到那个时候,我就可以更放心一点。"

❂ 西藏自治区扎西岗村村民罗桑旦达
Losang Tendar (right), a resident of Trashigang Village in Dagze County, Tibet Autonomous Region.

❂ 洛措带着罗桑来易地搬迁安置点
Lodra accompanies Losang Tendar to the new village.

TARGETED POVERTY ALLEVIATION

From November 3 to 5, 2013, President Xi Jinping inspected the poverty relief work in Hunan Province. Xi stressed that "to fight poverty in a targeted way, we must consider facts and local conditions rather than chanting slogans and setting goals beyond reach."

Over the past five years, an issue particularly important to Chinese President Xi Jinping has been poverty reduction. To address the issue, he has surveyed all 14 extremely poverty-stricken regions in China.

On average, China lifted 13.91 million people out of poverty annually over the past five years, over 55 million in total, which is about the population of a major European country.

On the path towards eradicating poverty and achieving common prosperity, China is leveraging its socialist system. The country's determination to eliminate poverty has composed a heartwarming page of human history.

国家开发银行负责的金融扶贫示范点
A pilot project of poverty alleviation through financial services operated by China Development Bank.

通过精准扶贫，贫困地区民众的收入水平逐渐提高
Thanks to targeted poverty alleviation, people in poverty-stricken areas have seen their incomes gradually increasing.

因地制宜，农民们有了新的致富渠道
Farmers explore new ways to get rich based on local conditions.

精准扶贫

扫码看本节短视频
Scan to watch the short video

2013年11月3日至5日，习近平主席考察湖南扶贫工作时说，我们在抓扶贫的时候，切忌喊大口号，也不要定那些好高骛远的目标。扶贫攻坚就是要实事求是，因地制宜，分类指导，精准扶贫。

这五年，习近平主席最关心的工作之一就是贫困人口脱贫，他走遍了、问遍了全国所有的十四个集中连片特困地区。

这五年，中国每年减贫一千三百九十一万人，累计脱贫五千五百多万人，相当于一个欧洲大国的人口。

消除贫困、共同富裕，中国正在践行着国家制度的本质要求。这宏大誓愿，是人类历史上温暖的一页。

2017年6月21日，山西省忻州市岢岚县赵家洼村的农民正在欢迎习近平主席进村走访
June 21, 2017: Farmers of Zhaojiawa Village in Kelan County, Xinzhou City, Shanxi Province, welcome President Xi Jinping during his visit to the village.

人民的生活越来越富裕，笑容洋溢在每一个人的脸上
People have smile on their face as they lead a better life.

THE "FUJIAN-NINGXIA COOPERATION MODEL"
FOR POVERTY ALLEVIATION

The vast territory of China is bestowed with diverse and varied landscapes. The divergences in natural endowment have also resulted in wide gaps between different parts of the country.

China is confident in its ability to provide solutions to make the weak strong.

The Fujian-Ningxia Cooperation Model is the epitome of China's paired poverty alleviation practice. So far, nine provinces (municipalites directly under the central government) and 13 major cities in east China have provided poverty relief aid for their respective sister provinces, autonomous regions and municipality directly under the central government in the west, covering all 30 autonomous prefectures mainly inhabited by ethnic minorities.

This is a major strategy to promote integrated, coordinated and common development of different regions, an important approach to strengthen regional cooperation and optimize industrial layout, and a significant measure to encourage rich regions to help impoverished areas and eventually achieve common prosperity.

The Fujian-Ningxia Model utilizes a Chinese solution to exploring a better social system for mankind and provides a vivid Chinese story of poverty alleviation for the world.

来闽宁镇兴建葡萄酒庄扶贫的福建企业家陈德启
Chen Deqi, an entrepreneur from Fujian Province who built wine chateaus in Minning Town, Ningxia Hui Autonomous Region, to help locals shake off poverty.

原隆村村民在葡萄园里工作
Farmers of Yuanlong Village work in a vineyard.

宁夏回族自治区闽宁镇戈壁滩
The desert land of Minning Town, Ningxia Hui Autonomous Region.

宁夏回族自治区闽宁镇的田园景色
The vast landscape of Minning Town, Ningxia Hui Autonomous Region.

On July 19, 2016, President Xi Jinping delivered a speech during his inspection tour of Ningxia. "I first visited this place in 1997. By then, Minning had implemented the poverty alleviation campaign of relocating impoverished villagers. Now, their annual average income has multiplied dozens of times (20 times, a villager interposed), from 500 yuan to more than 10,000 yuan. No one could achieve such a miracle except by following the leadership of the CPC and taking the socialist road. Stories like this testify to the superiority of our political system. Seeing people enjoy affluence and delight in happiness warms my heart. I want to thank you for all your efforts, which point us in the right direction towards common prosperity."

"I like the smell of the land here," grined Chen Deqi, a private entrepreneur from Fujian Province. "The untouched land emits a light but refreshing aroma. The area is located at 38.5 degrees North Latitude, the same as France, so it is suited for growing the best grapes to make the best wine."

"闽宁模式"
跨省市结对帮扶

扫码看本节短视频
Scan to watch the short video

辽阔的地理版图赋予了中国千姿百态的多样风光,自然禀赋的差异也同时形成了中国巨大的地域差异。

如何让羸弱变得强壮,中国有着自信的方案。

"闽宁模式"是中国跨省区市结对帮扶的一个缩影,东部九省和十三个城市与西部十个省区市已经结成对子,实现了对三十个民族自治州的帮扶全覆盖。

这是推动区域协调发展、协同发展、共同发展的大战略,是加强区域合作、优化产业布局的大手笔,是先富帮后富、最终实现共同富裕目标的大举措。

这是中国为人类探索更好社会制度提供的中国方案,也是当今世界最为生动的中国故事。

◉ 宁夏回族自治区闽宁镇的村庄
A village in Minning Town, Ningxia Hui Autonomous Region.

2016年7月19日,习近平主席在考察宁夏时说:"1997年我到这里,当时搞的这个移民吊庄工程,搞这个闽宁村,生活收入增长了几十倍呀,(村民插话:二十倍),五百块到现在一万多。这个只有谁能做到?只有共产党能够做,我们社会主义制度能够做,别的地方是做不成的,这个体现我们制度和政治的优越性,我看到你们这个生活,看到你们现在所洋溢的这种幸福感,我内心也感到很欣慰,这个也谢谢你们做的工作。你们做的工作,给我们指出了我们可以走的一条正确的康庄大道。"

福建民营企业家陈德启说:"我就喜欢这个地方的土地的味道,就是从来没有开垦过的一种清香味。这个地方的纬度,是跟法国一样的,三十八点五度,这个地方能种出最好的葡萄,能酿出最好的红酒。"

"习总书记就说,要号召福建这些闽商来宁夏这边发展,来闽宁镇上合作。我是2007年来的,那个时候来呢,就看上这片土地了。"

陈德启继续说道:"这戈壁滩你能干什么,可以说几千年来没有人在这个戈壁滩做什么东西,很

"President Xi Jinping called on Fujian business people to launch businesses in Ningxia, especially Minning Town," Chen recalled. "I came in 2007 because I saw plentiful opportunities on this land."

"At the time, many doubted the deserted land could produce anything," Chen said. "After all, few ever succeeded here. There were sure to be difficulties ahead–unusual difficulties. But unlike some, I stick to my goals after I decide on them. This is my innate personality."

Minning Town has become increasingly bustling over the past five years. Every day at 6 in the morning, many residents of the town's Yuanlong Village take a chartered bus to the vineyard to work. The new village has more than 10,000 residents, all of whom moved from Ningxia's poorest mountainous areas in 2012.

According to residents of Yuanlong Village of the Ningxia Hui Autonomous Region, they moved from a remote mountainous area where they could hardly make a living. "Now, life is becoming better and better with each passing day. We would not be leading such affluent lives without preferential policies implemented by the Party and the government. We feel happy from the bottom of our hearts."

Inspired by the Fujian-Ningxia Model, many impoverished areas in the Ningxia Hui Autonomous Region have transformed from deserted land to "gold". Over the past five years, the average income of rural residents in the autonomous region has increased by an annual rate of 10.7%.

宁夏原隆村村民们坐班车到葡萄园上班
Locals of Yuanlong Village in Ningxia Hui Autonomous Region waiting for a shuttle bus to the vineyard where they work.

多很多困难,不是一般的困难,但是呢,我这个人,有一个(地方)跟人家不一样,我不干的事,我就不做,我要做的事,我一定要做成,这就是我的个性。"

这五年,闽宁镇上更热闹了。每天早上六点,原隆村的村民们要坐上班车到葡萄园上班。这个移民新村里有一万多居民,都是2012年从宁夏最贫困的山区整村搬迁来的。

宁夏回族自治区原隆村村民说:"我们在老家那边山大沟深的,有时候一年苦着下来连肚子也吃不饱。现在生活一天比一天好,没有党、政府这么好的政策,我们生活也过不到这一步,真的心里特别高兴。"

从干沙滩变成金沙滩,在闽宁协作的带动下,五年来,宁夏农村居民的收入平均每年都能增长10.7%。

❀ 福建企业家在闽宁镇兴建的葡萄园
A vineyard built by a Fujian entrepreneur in Minning Town, Ningxia Hui Autonomous Region.

MUDU TOWN
THE STORY OF BALANCING URBAN AND RURAL DEVELOPMENT

A town with a history of more than 1,000 years in the suburb of Suzhou, Jiangsu Province, Mudu has become a role model for coordinated urban-rural development in China. Urban public services have expanded to Mudu, changing the lives of locals.

木渎，苏州城外的千年古镇
Mudu, an ancient town with a history of more than 1,000 years in the suburb of Suzhou, Jiangsu Province.

Gu Xuefeng, director of the Administrative Committee of the Jinqiao Development Zone in Mudu Town, Suzhou City, Jiangsu Province. "I'm not a native of Mudu. After graduating from college, I worked and lived in downtown Suzhou. Five years ago, I sold my house in downtown Suzhou and moved to Mudu with my family," Gu recounted. "Now we are all Mudu residents."

"Mudu is an inclusive place where everyone can find a platform to capitalize on their talent," Gu continued. "The local government provides plentiful opportunities for newcomers. People always find a way to make a decent living."

Five years ago, Mudu lacked elevated highways and subways, just like other nearby towns. Over the past couple of years, Mudu has been completely integrated into Suzhou. "In terms of industrial orientation, Mudu aims to serves as an industrial zone and a high-tech park for Suzhou. Anything you can find in downtown Suzhou can also be found in Mudu," Gu illustrated.

Mudu offers 114 one-stop public service items

木渎镇
城乡统筹发展的故事

木渎，苏州城外的千年古镇，中国城乡统筹画卷中的一道风景。城市的公共服务也在向这里延伸，改变着木渎人的生活。

交通越来越发达，千年古镇木渎正呈现出一番新气象
The millennium-old town of Mudu has taken a new look, with its transportation becoming increasingly convenient.

江苏省苏州市木渎镇金桥开发区管委会主任顾雪峰说："我不是木渎人。大学毕业以后，一直在苏州城里面工作。五年前，我把苏州城里面的房子卖掉了，全家举家迁到木渎来，所以说我们全家现在是新木渎人。"

"我说木渎是一个海纳百川的地方，你能在这个地方找到你发挥才能的平台，那么政府呢，也愿意把这些机会让新木渎人来做。要长久地生活下去，一定有你自己的舞台。"

"五年前木渎高架还没通，地铁还没通，应该来讲和其他乡镇没什么两样，但是这三年，木渎已经完全融入苏州了，我们木渎的产业定位就是承接着为苏州工业园区和苏州高新区配套的这么一个职能。你在苏州城里面有的东西，木渎都能解决。"

在木渎，无论是户籍、社保，还是企业办税，原先涉及十多个部门的一百一十四项公共服务，现在都能一站式办理。

顾雪峰说："政府在基础建设、新农村建设方面投入了好多钱，城乡一体化过程中间已经没有真

江苏省苏州市木渎镇金桥开发区管委会主任顾雪峰
Gu Xuefeng, director of the Administrative Committee of the Jinqiao Development Zone in Mudu Town, Suzhou City, Jiangsu Province.

木渎古镇美景
Beautiful scenery of Mudu town.

that originally involved a dozen departments such as household registration, social security and taxation for enterprises.

Gu Xuefeng says: "the local government has invested a huge volume of funds in infrastructure, especially in rural areas. Through integrated development of urban and rural areas, no more 'real farmers' can be found in Mudu. Rural residents also enjoy social security and medical insurance. In addition to the salary from his job, each resident also earns income from dividends paid to all villagers of Mudu. This gives locals a strong sense of gain."

"President Xi urges us to roll up our sleeves to forge ahead," Gu said. "To heed his call, we must take concrete action. Now is a golden age for China's development, as well as my personal salad days."

正意义上的农民了,社保、医保全部解决了,他除了工作以外,每年村里要给他一份分红。所以说,我们木渎老百姓他(们)这方面的获得感也很强。"

"总书记说,叫撸起袖子加油干,这种号召(要)落到我们的行动上。国家现在处于一个很好的时代,对我来讲,这也是赶上了一个好时代。"顾雪峰说。

❀ 木渎镇园林风光
A classical garden in Mudu Town.

❀ 木渎镇一站式办理服务百姓（组图）
Mudu Town offers one-stop administrative services for residents.

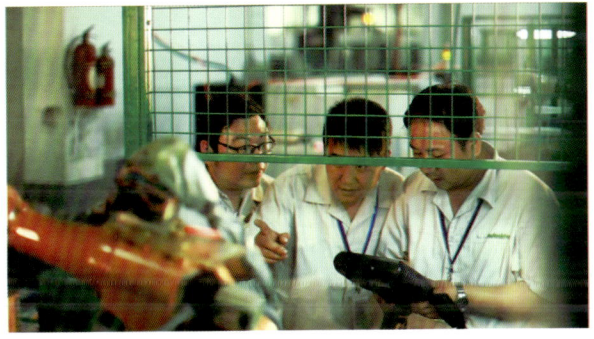

❀ 苏州市木渎镇金桥开发区（组图）
Jinqiao Development Zone in Mudu Town, Suzhou City, Jiangsu Province.

THE ESTABLISHMENT OF XIONG'AN NEW AREA

In 2016, the Beijing-Tianjin-Hebei region saw economic growth of 7.5% compared to the previous year and contributed 10% of China's total GDP. The region has become a major engine driving the country's economic development.

By breaking through the mindset of governance based on administrative division, the integrated development of Beijing, Tianjin and Hebei was upgraded to a national strategy with an aim to help the three places complement each other's advantages and achieve win-win cooperation. The strategy marks an innovation in methods to promote coordinated development.

In spring 2017, the Xiong'an New Area in Hebei Province was officially established.

On February 23, 2017, President Xi Jinping inspected Anxin County, Hebei Province. He presided over a seminar on the planning and construction of the Xiong'an New Area in the province. In his speech at the seminar, Xi pointed out that the Xiong'an New Area would be a historical legacy left for future generations and called for "world vision, international standards, Chinese characteristics and high goals" to build Xiong'an into "a demonstration area for innovative development".

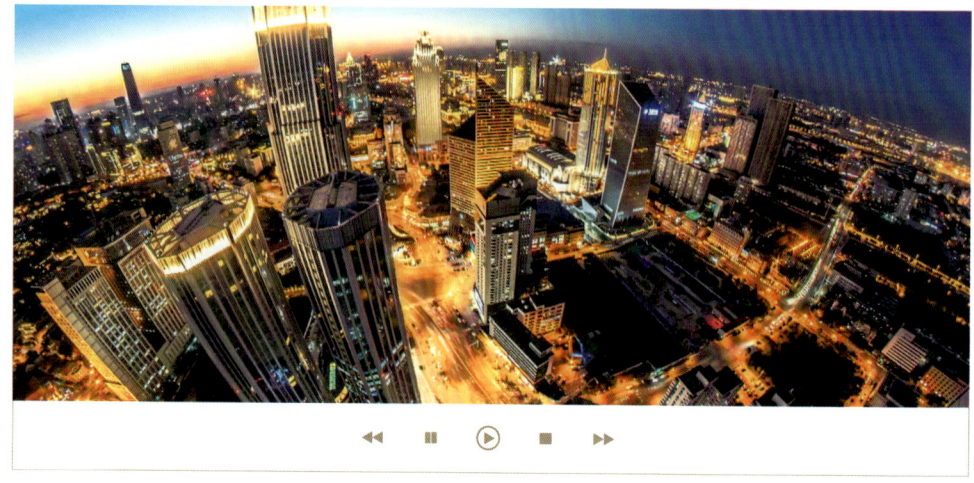

京津冀协同发展，优势互补、互利共赢
The integrated development of Beijing, Tianjin and Hebei aims to achieve complementary and win-win cooperation.

位于河北省保定市雄安新区境内的国家 5A 级旅游景区白洋淀
Baiyangdian Lake, a National 5A Scenic Area in Xiong'an New Area, Baoding City, Hebei Province.

设立雄安新区

扫码看本节短视频
Scan to watch the short video

❁ 2017年春天，雄安新区正式设立
Xiong'an New Area was officially founded in the spring of 2017.

2016年京津冀经济增速达到7.5%，经济规模占全国的10%，已经成为拉动中国经济发展的重要引擎。

打破"一亩三分地"的思维定势，将京津冀协同发展上升为国家战略，实现优势互补、互利共赢，这又是推进持续协调发展的一大创举。

2017年春天，雄安新区正式设立。

2017年2月23日，习近平主席在河北省安新县进行实地考察并主持召开河北雄安新区规划建设工作座谈会时说道："雄安新区将是我们留给子孙后代的历史遗产。必须坚持世界眼光、国际标准、中国特色、高点定位的理念，努力打造贯彻新发展理念的创新发展示范区。"

COORDINATED DEVELOPMENT OF THE FOUR REGIONS

A total of 14 Chinese cities have realized GDP surpassing one trillion yuan each. Meanwhile, the traditional provincial economy has begun to shift towards an economy based on central city clusters.

Measures have been taken to break traditional boundaries and remove administrative barriers.

China has unveiled a series of reforms and innovative measures to develop the western region, revitalize the northeastern region, promote the rise of the central region and enable the eastern region to spearhead development. Through coordinated development of the four regions, the entire country is moving towards common prosperity.

In September 2016, China promulgated Outline Plan on the Development of the Yangtze River Economic Belt. Spanning nine provinces and two municipalities directly under the central government, with a combined population of about 600 million, the economic belt is one of the largest and most influential inland river economic belts in the world, for which the Chinese government has clearly stressed the principle of "prioritizing ecological protection while avoiding large-scale development."

China is leveraging visionary top-level design to break the "curses" of its economic development.

This can be attributed to China's institutional confidence. This is a miracle with distinctive Chinese characteristics.

广州，中国经济崛起的急先锋，中心城市群建设风景独好
A central city in the Pearl River Delta, Guangzhou is a forerunner in economic development of China.

北京，中心城市群道路建设环环紧扣，仿佛一条条珍珠项链，把首都北京装点得更加美丽
Beijing boasts modern ring roads that circle like pearl necklaces, adding unrivaled beauty to the capital.

青岛，近年来中心城市群变化引人瞩目，东方之星冉冉升起
As a central city on the Shandong Peninsula, Qingdao has risen like a shining star in eastern China in recent years.

西子湖畔的杭州向世界展示了古典之美与现代之光，杭州点击鼠标联通的将是整个世界
Hangzhou, located on the banks of West Lake, showcases classical beauty and modern appeal to the world. A city noted for its internet companies, Hangzhou is connected to the outside world with a click of the mouse.

四大板块协调发展

中国已有十四座城市跻身 GDP 万亿之列，而中国传统的省域经济也开始向中心城市群经济转变。

打破传统的界限，消除行政的藩篱。

西部开发、东北振兴、中部崛起、东部率先，四大板块协调发展、协同发展、共同发展的战略进一步推进。

2016 年 9 月，《长江经济带发展规划纲要》公布，九省两市，约六亿人口，这是目前世界上可开发规模最大、影响范围最广的内河经济带，中国已明确提出"共抓大保护，不搞大开发"。

中国正在用大手笔的顶层设计打破经济发展的"魔咒"。

这是中国制度带来的自信，这是中国特色书写的传奇！

中国传统的省域经济，也开始向中心城市群经济转变。组图为各地城市新貌
Modern cities in China. The traditional provincial economy has begun to shift towards an economy based on central city clusters in the country.

中国力量 THE CHINESE STRENGTH

上海，中心城市群发展先行、先试，勇立改革潮头
Riding the tide of reform, Shanghai is a forerunner in the development of central city clusters in China.

扫码看同内容电影
Scan to watch the film

扫码看同类专题片
Scan to watch similar documentaries

第四章

▶ 绿色中国
Ⅳ A GREENER CHINA

2017年10月18日，习近平总书记在中国共产党第十九次全国代表大会上说，生态文明建设功在当代、利在千秋。建设生态文明是中华民族永续发展的千年大计。必须树立和践行绿水青山就是金山银山的理念。

今天的中国，正在像对待生命一样对待生态环境。

绿色已经成为中国发展的新理念。

On October 18, 2017, General Secretary and Chinese President Xi Jinping said at the 19th CPC National Congress that work done today to build an ecological civilization will benefit generations to come. Building an ecological civilization is vital to sustaining the Chinese nation's development. We must realize that lucid waters and lush mountains are invaluable assets and act on this understanding.

In today's China, people treat the environment as they treat their own lives.

Green development has become a new vision for future China.

THE ESTABLISHMENT OF NATURE RESERVES

The concept of green development is increasingly popular, and the action of building a beautiful China is constantly upgrading and speeding up. China, with blue sky, green earth and clear water, is coming back to us.

活动在玛旁雍错湿地的藏羚羊
Tibetan antelopes in the Mapham Yutso Lake wetland.

普兰县林业局副局长才旺丹加正在玛旁雍错湿地观察藏羚羊
Tsewang Dongyal monitors Tibetan antelopes living in the Mapham Yutso Lake wetland.

As the kidney of earth, wetland is an irreplaceable ecosystem for species storage and climate regulation. Over the past five years, China's wetland reserves have increased in number from 553 to 602, and a national wetland conservation system has taken shape.

Meanwhile, 85% of the wild animal population and 65% of higher plant communities in China have been effectively protected over the past five years.

The country is becoming greener and more vibrant with life.

Tsewang Dongyal, deputy director of the Forestry Bureau of Burang County, Ngari, Tibet Autonomous Region. He said that the central government and the local government of Tibet both attach great importance to wetland ecological conservation. In 2010, the Mapham Yutso Lake in Burang County became a nature reserve at the the autonomous regional level. Since 2012, surveys have been conducted each year to monitor the population of Tibetan antelopes in the nature reserve.

According to Tsewang Dongyal, the Mapham Yutso Lake wetland is an important and irreplaceable passage for the migration of Tibetan antelopes. "In 2012, some 1,600 Tibetan antelopes were monitored in the area, and the figure increased to more than 2,200 last year," he said, adding: "The population of the animal is likely to continue expanding in the years to come."

"I'm delighted and proud that so few poaching cases have occurred over the past few years," said Dongyal.

In addition, the Bayanbulak Grassland in the Xinjiang Uygur Autonomous Region, which once faced the threat of economical degradation, is becoming green again.

More than 7,200 local herders have become full-time protectors of the Sanjiangyuan National Nature Reserve deep on the Qinghai-Tibet Plateau. Wild animals dubbed "fairies of plateau" such as snow leopards and lynxes have started returning to the nature reserve.

The area where the Yangtze, Yellow and Lancang rivers originate has seen its water resources increasing by 8.4 billion cubic meters and its wetlands expanding by 104 square kilometers.

A photo of a Northeast Panther which is one of the world's most endangered large cats was taken by an infrared camera in the forest of the Changbai Mountains.

The Qinling Mountains are home to more than 300 wild pandas. It is where the world's first and only brown-colored wild panda was discovered.

Every creature subsists and prospers at the mercy of Mother Nature.

建设自然保护区

扫码看本节短视频
Scan to watch the short video

绿色发展的理念日益深入人心，建设美丽中国的行动不断升级提速。一个天蓝、地绿、水清的中国正在重回身边，重现眼前。

❀ 内蒙古自治区库布齐沙漠变绿洲
The Kubuqi Desert in the Inner Mongolia Autonomous Region has been transformed into an oasis.

被称为"地球之肾"的湿地是物种栖息、气候调节不可替代的一种生态系统。中国的湿地自然保护区已经从五年前的五百五十三个增加到六百零二个，全国性的湿地保护体系初见规模。

这五年，中国85%的野生动物种群、65%的高等植物群落都得到了有效保护。

绿色，让生命跳动。

西藏自治区阿里地区普兰县林业局副局长才旺丹加说："国家和自治区都很重视湿地生态保护。我们那个普兰县的玛旁雍错，2010年的时候就升为自治区保护级别了，自2012年开始，每年（我们）都要下去监测藏羚羊的数量。"

"玛旁雍错湿地对于藏羚羊迁徙来说，它是一个重要的通道，也是唯一的一个通道。2012年的时候，我们监测到了不到一千六百只（藏羚羊），去年的统计数量是有两千两百多只，再过几年的话，可能还会持续增长吧。"

"近几年，基本上没发生过那种人类去捕猎啊、偷猎啊（的事情）。没发生过那种案子，我很自豪。"才旺丹加说。

除此之外，新疆维吾尔族自治区巴音布鲁克草原上，曾一度面临退化危机的草场正在变绿。

青藏高原腹地，七千二百多名牧民组成的专职管护员守护的三江源，雪豹、猞猁这些高原精灵又回来了。

长江、黄河、澜沧江流淌过的这片土地，水资源量增加八十四亿立方米、湿地面积增加一百零四平方公里。

长白山珲春的森林里，远红外相机捕捉到了全球极度濒危的大型猫科动物东北豹的身影。

秦岭山脉，野生大熊猫的乐园。三百多只野生大熊猫在这里生活，人们在这里发现了目前全球唯一一只野生棕色大熊猫。

万物各得其和以生，各得其养以成。

中国力量 THE CHINESE STRENGTH

THE MAPHAM YUTSO LAKE WETLAND IN THE TIBET AUTONOMOUS REGION

⊛ 广阔的西藏自治区玛旁雍错湿地风光
The magnificent landscape of the Mapham Yutso Lake wetland.

⊛ 修复后的西藏自治区玛旁雍错湿地（组图）
The Mapham Yutso Lake wetland after ecological restoration.

西藏自治区玛旁雍错湿地

◈ 西藏自治区玛旁雍错湿地里生活的水鸟
　Water birds living in the Mapham Yutso Lake wetland, Tibet Autonomous Region.

◈ 玛旁雍错湿地环境变好，水鸟们在此栖息
　A number of water birds have settled in the Mapham Yutso Lake wetland as its ecological environment gets better.

THE BAYANBULAK GRASSLAND IN THE XINJIANG UYGUR AUTONOMOUS REGION

◉ 新疆维吾尔自治区巴音布鲁克草原正在变绿
The Bayanbulak Grassland in the Xinjiang Uygur Autonomous Region, which once faced the threat of economical degradation, is becoming green again.

新疆维吾尔自治区巴音布鲁克草原

◉ 美丽的新疆巴音布鲁克草原景色
The beautiful Bayanbulak Grassland in the Xinjiang Uygur Autonomous Region.

◉ 草原上的羊群与骏马
Sheep and horses grazing on the grassland.

中国力量 THE CHINESE STRENGTH

THE SANJIANGYUAN NATIONAL NATURE RESERVE IN SOUTHERN QINGHAI PROVINCE

❀ 青海南部三江源国家级自然保护区美丽风光
The beautiful landscape of the Sanjiangyuan National Nature Reserve in southern Qinghai Province.

青海南部三江源国家级自然保护区

◎ 青海南部三江源国家级自然保护区内人与动物和谐相处
　 Humans and wild animals coexist in harmony at the Sanjiangyuan National Nature Reserve in southern Qinghai Province.

ANIMALS LIVING IN NATURE RESERVES

陕西省秦岭地区发现的野生棕色大熊猫
The brown wild giant panda discovered in Qinling Mountains, Shaanxi Province.

陕西省秦岭地区的自然保护区内，大熊猫在此栖息
The Qinling Mountains nature reserve in Shaanxi Province is a habitat for giant pandas.

自然保护区内的动物

❀ 自然保护区内人与动物和谐相处
Humans and wild animals coexist in harmony at the national nature reserve.

MARINE ECOLOGICAL RESTORATION

Upholding the new principle of classified land administration, China has defined "three lines" – the ecological conservation red line, the environmental quality baseline, and the upper resource usage limit line. As a community of shared life, mountains, rivers, forests, croplands, lakes and grasslands are no longer administrated separately.

Over the past five years, China has invested a total of 110 billion yuan in marine ecological restoration.

The percentage of the country's offshore areas with above-standard water quality has rebounded from 62.8% to 73.4%.

China's marine development mode has shifted towards recycled utilization.

Its efforts to protect the ocean have been rewarded with clear seawater, blue skies and clean beaches.

The ecological restoration efforts of Sansha City, Hainan Province, have expanded from land to sea.

The beautiful city of Sansha in Hainan Province boasts blue sky and clear sea.

修复海洋生态

扫码看本节短视频
Scan to watch the short video

在国土空间分类管制的新理念中,中国制定了三条红线:生态功能的保障基线、环境质量的安全底线、自然资源的利用上线。"山水林田湖草"作为生命共同体,终于不再被人为割裂开来。

最近五年,中国修复海洋生态总投入超过一千一百亿元。

全国近岸海域水质优良比例,五年来从 62.8% 回升到了 73.4%。

中国的海洋开发方式正在向循环利用型转变。

这碧海蓝天、洁净沙滩,就是它给予的最好回报与馈赠。

❀ 修复后的海洋更加适合海洋生物的生存(组图)
The restored marine ecosystem is more suitable for sea animals.

中国力量 THE CHINESE STRENGTH

🌺 海南省三沙市近年来开展海洋生态修复，图为当地美丽的三沙晋卿岛
The beautiful Jinqing Island in Sansha City, Hainan Province. In recent years, Sansha has implemented a campaign to restore its marine ecosystem.

THE DEVELOPMENT OF GREEN ENERGY

In today's China, people treat the environment as they treat their own lives. Green development has become a new vision for future China.

On average, two wind turbines are installed each hour in China, making the country a leader in the global wind power market.

On average, solar panels with combined surface space of a football field are installed each hour around China. Today, China has become the world's largest photovoltaic power producer.

The Hualong One Nuclear Power Plant was independently designed and constructed by China, and its technologies have been exported to Britain and Argentina. Moreover, more than 20 countries have expressed intentions to cooperate with the power plant.

The Xiluodu Hydropower Station in Sichuan Province has won the FIDIC award, which is considered the Nobel Prize of international engineering consulting.

位于福建省福清市建设中的东南沿海"华龙一号"核电站，使用的是我国具有完整自主知识产权的第三代核电技术
The Hualong One Nuclear Power Plant under construction in Fuqing City, Fujian Province, on the southeast coast of China. The power station adopts the third-generation nuclear power technology that China owns independent intellectual property right.

青海省格尔木共和光伏电站
Gonghe Photovoltaic Power Station in Golmud, Qinghai Province.

甘肃省敦煌 100 兆瓦熔盐塔式光热电站局部图
Partial photo of a 100MW molten salt tower photo-thermal power station in Dunhuang, Gansu Province.

发展绿色能源

今天的中国正在像对待生命一样对待生态环境。绿色已经成为中国发展的新理念。

中国每小时就有两座风机安装到位。在全球风电市场，中国遥遥领先。

中国每小时就有一座足球场面积大小的太阳能电池板被安装上。中国已经是世界光伏第一大国。

中国自主研发的"华龙一号"核电站已经建成。"华龙一号"技术已经出口到英国、阿根廷，还有二十多个国家提出合作意向。

四川溪洛渡水电站还获得了工程界的"诺贝尔奖"。

扫码看本节短视频
Scan to watch the short video

草原上的风力发电机组
Wind turbines on the grassland.

获得国际工程大奖的四川溪洛渡水电站
The Xiluodu Hydropower Station in Sichuan Province has won an international engineering award.

中国力量 THE CHINESE STRENGTH

甘肃省敦煌 100 兆瓦熔盐塔式光热电站
A 100MW molten salt tower photo-thermal power station in Dunhuang, Gansu Province.

5兆瓦海上风电机组
A 5MW marine wind turbine.

LUCID WATERS AND LUSH MOUNTAINS ARE INVALUABLE ASSETS

China has since 2013 enacted a series of regulations to limit air, water and soil pollution, heralding the beginning of China's largest-scale battle against pollution.

Over the past five years, the central government of China has invested a total of 36.3 billion yuan in a campaign to restore cultivated land to forest. During the period, the country has added nearly 30 million hectares of artificial forests, an increase of 21.3% on five years ago. Now, China's total area of artificial forests has reached 69.3 million hectares, ranking first in the world.

The environment concerns people's well-being. Green mountains and blue skies foster beautiful, happy lives. Chinese people now have greater aspirations for a prosperous lives.

鸟瞰黄土高原壮丽风光
A bird's-eye view of the magnificent Loess Plateau.

Kubuqi Desert is in the Inner Mongolia Autonomous Region. It used to be a source of sandstorms plaguing the Beijing-Tianjin-Hebei region. Now, it's not only greenery, but also has greenhouses, with more than 100 species of seedlings to be planted in the desert.

Area of desertified land in China decreases by 1,980 square kilometers annually, and the Kubuqi has been hailed by UN Environment Program (UNEP) as a global role model for desertification control.

The Loess Plateau has constantly pressed ahead with a project to restore cultivated land back to forests and pastures, expanding the vegetated land of Shaanxi Province northwards by 400 kilometers.

Saihanba Forest Farm is in Chengde City, Hebei Province. The forest farm of nearly 75,000 hectares is the world's largest artificial forest. Thanks to persistent efforts, three generations of workers in Saihanba Forest Farm created an epic of ecological conservation in contemporary China, for which they were honored with the Champions of the Earth Award by UNEP.

"When we plant green seedlings, we sow the seeds

绿水青山就是金山银山

扫码看本节短视频
Scan to watch the short video

从 2013 年开始,"大气十条""水十条""土十条"接连出台,中国发起了史上最大规模的污染治理之战。

这五年来,中央对新一轮退耕还林投资累计超过三百六十三亿元,全国新造人工林四亿四千七百万亩,比五年前增长了 21.3%。中国人工林总面积已达十亿四千万亩,位居全球之首。

环境就是民生,青山就是美丽,蓝天也是幸福。中国人对小康生活已经有了更多美好的期待。

❀ 黄土高原持续实施的退耕还林还草工程
The Loess Plateau has constantly pressed ahead with a project to turn croplands back to forests and pastures in recent years.

❀ 河北省承德市塞罕坝机械林场原职工陈彦娴
Chen Yanxian, a former employee of the Saihanba Forest Farm in Chengde City, Hebei Province.

内蒙古自治区的库布齐沙漠曾经是京津冀地区沙尘暴的源头之一,现在,这里不仅变绿了,还盖了花房,有一百多种苗木等待栽种。

中国沙化土地年均缩减一千九百八十平方公里,被联合国环境规划署盛赞为全球沙漠治理的典范。

黄土高原持续实施的退耕还林还草工程,让陕西的绿色版图向北推进了四百公里。

河北省承德市塞罕坝人工林场的一百一十二万亩林海是世界上最大的人工林。坝上三代人,用愚公移山的精神在荒原上创造了属于中国生态保护的

◎ 大兴安岭林场
A forest farm in the Greater Khingan Mountains.

of hope for a beautiful future," said Chen Yanxian, a former employee of the Saihanba Forest Farm.

Chinese people now have greater aspirations for a prosperous lives.

On March 29, 2017, Chinese President Xi Jinping attended a tree planting activity in Beijing, at which he called for building a green shelter for future generations. "The people should live in green shade, which is the target of our efforts," Xi declared. "We need to roll up our sleeves and keep working year after year, generation after generation."

At the APEC welcome banquet on November 11, 2014, President Xi expressed hoped that Beijing and even China would retain blue skies, green mountains and clear rivers, so that children can live in a sound ecological environment, which is an important aspect of the Chinese Dream.

◈ 自然环境越来越好，绿水青山常在
China's natural environment has constantly improved, enabling people to enjoy clear waters and lush mountains.

当代史诗，无愧于联合国授予的"地球卫士奖"。

塞罕坝机械林场原职工陈彦娴说："我们相信种下绿色就能收获美丽，种下希望就能收获未来。"

中国人对小康生活已经有了更多美好的期待。

2017年3月29日，习近平主席参加首都义务植树活动时说："要培育这年轻一代了，要建立绿色屏障。人们都应该生活在绿荫之中，所以这些是我们努力的方向。一年接着一年干，一代接着一代干，撸起袖子加油干。"

2014年11月10日，习近平主席在APEC欢迎宴会上致辞时就说过，我希望北京乃至全中国都能够蓝天常在、青山常在、绿水常在，让孩子们都生活在良好的生态环境之中，这也是中国梦中很重要的内容。

位于河北、内蒙古交界的塞罕坝机械林场，经过三代建设者的不懈努力，已经成为世界上面积最大的人工林海。今天的塞罕坝不再以木材产业为主导，而是发展了苗木、风电、旅游等多种经营方式

After unremitting efforts of three generations, the Saihanba Forest Farm on the border between Hebei Province and Inner Mongolia Autonomous Region has become the world's largest artificial forest. Today, the forest farm has no longer depended on the logging industry, but developed a variety of industries such as seedling cultivation, wind power, and tourism.

扫码看同内容电影
Scan to watch the film

扫码看同类专题片
Scan to watch similar documentaries

第五章

▶ 共享小康
Ⅴ SHARED PROSPERITY

2012年11月15日,在中共十八届中央政治局常委同中外记者见面会上,习近平总书记说:"我们的人民热爱生活,期盼有更好的教育、更稳定的工作、更满意的收入、更可靠的社会保障、更高水平的医疗卫生服务、更舒适的居住条件、更优美的环境,期盼着孩子们能成长得更好、工作得更好、生活得更好。人民对美好生活的向往,就是我们的奋斗目标。"

On November 15, 2012 while leading the newly elected members of the Standing Committee of the 18th CPC Central Committee Political Bureau to meet the press, CPC General Secretary and Chinese President Xi Jinping said: "Our people have an ardent love for life. They want to have better education, more stable jobs, more income, reliable social security, better medical and health care, improved housing conditions and a beautiful environment. They hope that their children will have sound growth, good jobs and more enjoyable lives. The people's wish for a happy life is our mission."

THE REVITALIZATION OF EDUCATION

Since ancient times, Chinese parents have done all they can to help their children receive better education, even in poverty-stricken families. Education is an essential weapon to shake off poverty.

In 2015, the Chinese government launched the first-ever rural teacher support program since 1949, which helps more than 3 million rural teachers to lead more decent and dignified lives.

Meanwhile, the Chinese government launched the free lunch program, which provides a four-yuan meal allowance per day for 36 million students in rural China.

Government education expenditures in China have surpassed 4% of the country's GDP for five consecutive years. In 2016, the amount exceeded 3 trillion yuan for the first time, increasing by 1.3 trillion yuan compared to five years ago.

The future's arms are wide open for those lovely children.

From the "First Class of the New Semester" for younger students to the "Leaving the Best Memories of Alma Maters" for college graduates and the selection of the "Most Beautiful Rural Teachers," a series of campaigns have been carried out in China. Pursuit of beauty and kindness is a common aspiration of all of society. Honoring martyrs demonstrates respect and esteem for heroes who sacrificed their lives for the nation and the people.

Moral integrity is essential for both a noble man and a prosperous nation. It has served as a solid foundation for the development of the Chinese nation.

孩子们开心地去上学。据教育部发布的《2018年全国教育事业发展统计公报》显示，2018年全国小学学龄儿童净入学率达到99.95%

Children on their way to school. According to the 2018 Statistical Report on Education Development in China released by the Ministry of Education, the country's net enrollment rate of school-agers in primary schools reached 99.95% in 2018.

放学归来的学生们。据教育部官网公布，2018年全国九年制义务教育巩固率达94.2%

Students on their way home. Statistics published on the official website of China's Ministry of Education show that the cohort survival rate in nine-year compulsory education in the country reached 94.2% in 2018.

振兴教育

扫码看本节短视频
Scan to watch the short video

中国人有"家贫子读书"的传统,摆脱贫困的第一步,就是有文化。

2015年,中国通过了中华人民共和国历史上第一个乡村教师队伍支持计划,三百多万乡村教师有了更体面、更有尊严的生活。

每人补助四块钱,免费午餐的国家工程,已经惠及全国三千六百万农村学生。

中国的教育经费总投入,已经连续五年占GDP的4%以上。2016年首次超过三万亿,比五年前增长了一点三万亿元。

未来,在向这些可爱的孩子们招手。

从小学生的"开学第一课",到大学毕业生"留给母校最美的背影",以及"最美乡村教师"等"最美系列"评选,让寻找最美、成为最美,变成全社会的追求。一个个英雄楷模的树立,是对国家功勋、人民功勋的敬仰和尊重。

国无德不兴,人无德不立,这是中华民族强基固本的基础。

❀ 即将完成学业的高校学生。据教育部官网公布,2018年全国普通本专科毕业生达753.31万人
College students about to graduate. Statistics published on the official website of China's Ministry of Education show that more than 7.53 million college students graduated around the country in 2018.

❀ 图书馆里坐满了学习的青年
Young people studying at a library.

❀ 小学生身穿中国传统服饰迎来"开学第一课"
Primary school students in traditional Chinese attire attend their "first class" on the School Opening Day.

❀ 在2012年中央电视台"寻找最美乡村教师"颁奖典礼现场,学生们向获奖老师敬礼
Students saluting to award-winning teachers at the award ceremony of the "Most Beautiful Rural Teachers" launched by CCTV in 2012.

中国力量 THE CHINESE STRENGTH

DING BAOHUA, A TEACHER IN A VILLAGE SCHOOL DEEP IN MOUNTAINS

安徽省六安市金寨县沙河乡垒峰村地处大别山腹地，在这里教了三十八年书的丁保花，既是孩子们的老师，也是孩子们的妈妈
Ding Baohua, who has taught in the school of Leifeng Village hidden deep in the Dabie Mountains, in Shahe Township, Jinzhai County, Anhui Province, for 38 years, is more than just a teacher. Many students call her "mother".

丁保花在为孩子们上课
Ding Baohua gives lessons at class.

丁保花送孩子们回家
Ding Baohua escorts students on their way home.

大山里的教师丁保花

☯ 垒峰村学生夏桂林为奶奶盛菜，因为贫困，夏桂林的妈妈生下她就离开了大山
Xia Guilin, a student in Leifeng Village, Anhui Province, takes care of his grandmother. Suffering from poverty, his mother left home to work elsewhere soon after he was born.

☯ 丁保花班上的孩子们在认真听课
Students at a class taught by Ding Baohua.

☯ 免费午餐惠及越来越多的孩子，垒峰村的孩子们都能吃到热乎乎的午餐
The "Free Lunch" program has benefited increasing numbers of children. Now children in Leifeng Village are access to lunch for free at school.

☯ 上美术课的孩子们在外写生
A child sketching from nature at an outdoor art class.

THE PROSPERITY OF CULTURE

Traditional Chinese culture is gaining a new look by keeping abreast of the times. Aspirations for national rejuvenation have been implanted in the heart of every Chinese person.

In his speech at the 19th CPC National Congress on October 18, 2017, General Secretary and Chinese President Xi Jinping said: "Cultural confidence represents a fundamental and profound force that sustains the development of a country and a nation." "We will draw on China's fine traditional culture, keep alive and develop its vision, concepts, values, and moral norms, and do so in a way that responds to the call of our era. With this we will see that Chinese culture maintains its appeal and evolves with the times."

To date, 39 Chinese items have been inscribed on the World Intangible Cultural Heritage list.

In 2016, the annual added value of China's cultural industry surpassed 3 trillion yuan, increasing by 67.4% from 2012, with its percentage in GDP exceeding 4% for the first time.

Radio and television services serve more than 98% of China's total population. Each year, China produces nearly 15,000 episodes of television dramas.

In 2017, China's box office revenues hit 55 billion yuan, making the country the world's second-largest film market. The number of cinema screens in China exceeds 50,000, more than in all of North America.

Summarizing core socialist values aims to reach great consensus on the cultural values of the Chinese nation.

On February 28, 2015 at the fourth awards conference for national civilized cities, towns and institutions and advanced representatives in juvenile moral education, Chinese President Xi Jinping said that the Chinese people's ideals give the country its strength and creates a bright future for the nation.

A culturally advanced society is taking shape in China, with the Chinese spirit showcased on the smiling face of every Chinese citizen.

竹简形式的大型雕塑向人们解读着社会主义核心价值观的内涵
A large sculpture resembling bamboo slips interprets the content of China's core socialist values.

中国传统艺术形式——书法
Calligraphy, a traditional writing art of China.

繁荣文化

扫码看本节短视频
Scan to watch the short video

中国传统文化与时代精神正焕发出新的面貌，将复兴之魂厚植于心。

2017年10月18日，习近平总书记在中国共产党第十九次全国代表大会上说："文化自信是一个国家、一个民族发展中更基本、更深沉、更持久的力量。深入挖掘中华优秀传统文化蕴含的思想观念、人文精神、道德规范，结合时代要求继承创新，让中华文化展现出永久魅力和时代风采。"

中国已经有三十九个项目被列为世界级非物质文化遗产。

2016年，中国文化产业年增加值突破三万亿元，比2012年增长了67.4%，占GDP比重首次超过4%。

广播电视人口综合覆盖率超过98%。电视剧年产量近一万五千集。

2017年，中国电影票房突破五百五十亿，已是全球第二大电影市场，银幕数突破五万块，超过了整个北美地区的银幕数量总和。

社会主义核心价值观的概括，找到了中华民族精神价值追求的最大公约数。

2015年2月28日，在第四届全国文明城市、文明村镇、文明单位和未成年人思想道德建设工作先进代表表彰大会上，习近平主席说，人民有信仰，民族才有希望，国家才有力量。

文化小康正在绽放，中国精神正洋溢在每一个中国人的笑脸上。

城市街头的社会主义核心价值观内容展示
A sculpture displaying the content of China's core socialist values on the street.

WORLD INTANGIBLE CULTURAL HERITAGE IN CHINA

◈ 中国的世界级非物质文化遗产之川剧变脸
The mask-changing show of Sichuan Opera is a world-renowned intangible cultural heritage in China.

◈ 从雕刻到泥塑，许多承载着中国传统文化的手工艺瑰宝已被收入世界级非物质文化遗产名录中（组图）
Many handicrafts bearing testimony to traditional Chinese culture and art, including carving and clay sculpture, have been inscribed on the World Intangible Cultural Heritage List.

中国"非遗"

◈ 中国的世界级非物质文化遗产之武当武术
 Wudang Martial Arts are a world-renowned intangible cultural heritage in China.

◈ 舞龙、舞狮均是独具中国特色的古老习俗，随着国际文化交流的日渐频繁，它们也逐渐成为中国文化的代表之一（组图）
 As traditional performing arts with Chinese flavor, dragon dance and lion dance have gradually become icons of Chinese culture with the flourishing of international cultural exchanges.

A CULTURALLY ADVANCED SOCIETY

从京剧到各民族传统舞蹈,中国人民可参与并观赏到丰富多彩的文艺表演(组图)
From Peking Opera to traditional ethnic dances, Chinese people can participate in and enjoy various art performances.

文化小康

◎ 电影市场日趋繁荣，2018 年全国银幕总数已突破六万块，稳居世界电影银幕数量首位
China's film market has boomed. In 2018, the number of cinema screens in China exceeded 60,000, ranking first around the world.

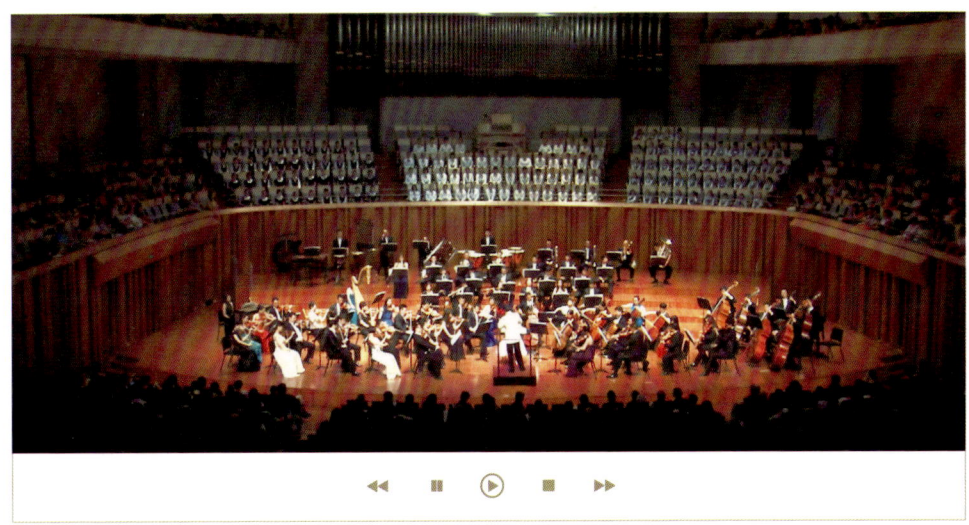

◎ 音乐会等演出越来越多，据《2018 年文化和旅游发展统计公报》显示，2018 年全年艺术表演团体共演出 312.46 万场
Art performances such as concerts have been increasing in China. According to the *2018 Statistical Report on Cultural and Tourism Development of China*, art troupes in the country presented a more than 3.12 million performances in 2018.

MEDICAL SERVICES ARE ACCESSIBLE TO ALL

Over the past five years, China has carried out a comprehensive reform of public hospitals. China has provided critical illness insurance for more than a billion urban and rural residents. A total of 205 cities in the country explored the new model of "Conjoined Twins", which encourages famous physicians from large hospitals to regularly provide services in community-level clinics.

Protecting public health demonstrates respect for life and enables the ancient Chinese civilization to thrive forever.

全国实施城乡居民大病保险
China has provided critical illness insurance for both urban and rural residents.

医院的自助挂号机。随着科技的发展，挂号看病也越来越快捷便利
Self-help hospital registration machine. The advancement of science and technology had made seeing doctor more convenient than before.

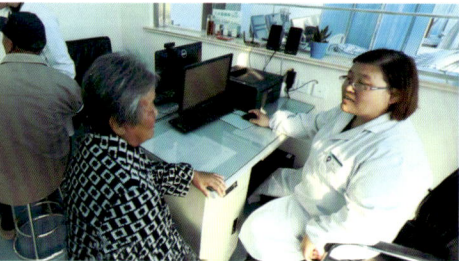

大医院名医到社区诊所出诊，为居民提供方便
Many medical experts from prestigious hospitals regularly serve in community hospitals for convenience of local residents.

病有所医

扫码看本节短视频
Scan to watch the short video

这五年，中国全面推行公立医院综合改革。实施城乡居民大病保险，覆盖人群超过十亿。全国两百零五个城市探索"医联体"新模式，大医院的名医出现在社区诊所。

对健康的护佑，对生命的尊重，让古老中国的文明永续繁衍。

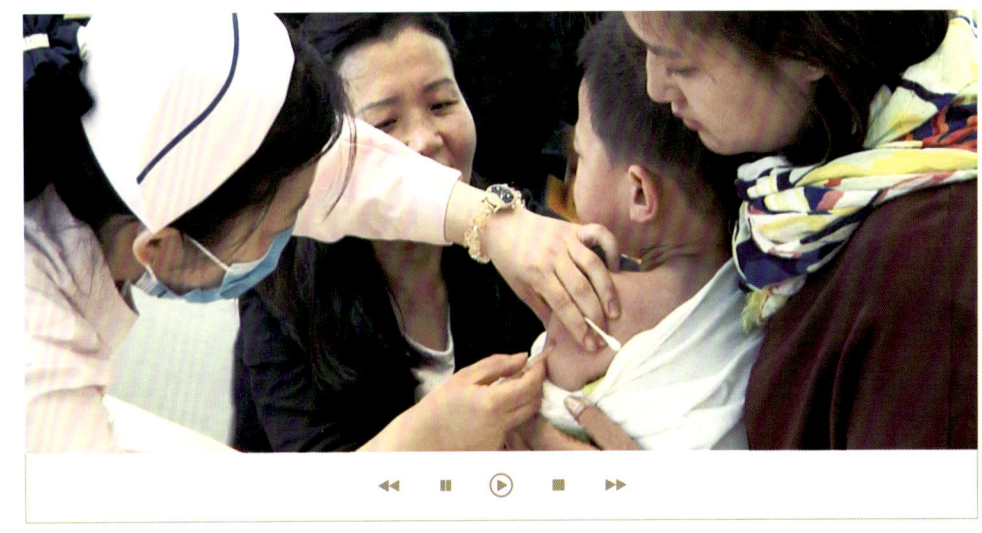

❀ 给儿童接种疫苗
　Vaccinating a child.

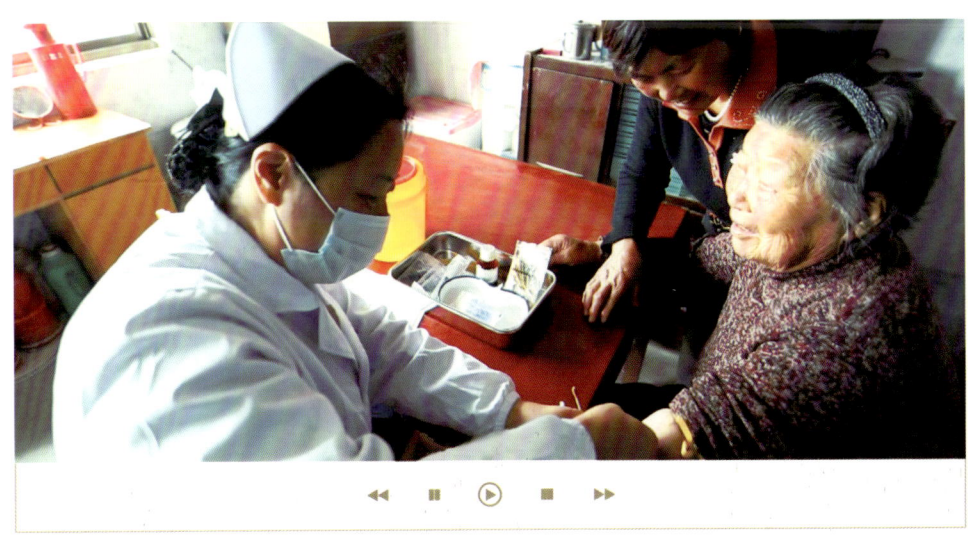

❀ 为老年人诊疗
　Diagnosing an old patient.

FAMILY DOCTORS

Seeing a family doctor is not a privilege of the noble in China. As a country with a population of more than 1.3 billion, China is determined to ensure everyone has access to improved public medical services. This is a promise made by the government.

To optimize the allocation of medical resources, the city of Xiamen in Fujian Province established a hierarchical medical care system. Starting with chronic diseases such as diabetes and hypertension that are common among inpatients visiting large hospitals, the city implemented a service model featuring a combined team comprised of "three kinds of medical professionals," namely, medical specialists at hospitals, community-level family doctors, and health management worker who together provide medical and healthcare services for residents. Of 38 publicly-run community-level medical care institutions, the Gulangyu Hospital under the No.1 Hospital Affiliated to Xiamen University was ranked first at the annual assessment in 2016.

On the business card of Yang Yan, a health management worker at the Gulangyu Hospital, it is said: "5+2, day and night. Monitoring your health conditions 24 hours a day." One day, she came to Cai Baorui's house. According to Cai Baorui, a resident of Gulangyu Islet, her husband suffered hematuria on New Year's Eve which was extremely painful. Fortunately, she could contact Yang Yan immediately whenever her husband felt sick, and Yang would arrange for him to be treated by doctors at a top-level hospital.

"She is even dearer than my own daughter," Cai Baorui remarked. "Her considerate services make me feel assured and safe. Now, I'm happy every day of the year. The Party is attaching greater importance to the care of the elderly. Living in such a peaceful and prosperous era, we will undoubtedly enjoy longer lives."

Yang Yan considers health management workers like her a bridge between residents and general practitioners. "This is why we need to visit local households frequently to establish close communication to get as detailed health information as possible," she explained.

China has set the goal of achieving full coverage of the contracted family doctor system by 2020, so that every Chinese citizen will have a family doctor. The goal has been included in the "Healthy China 2030" Plan, the world's largest health program. China has formed the world's largest basic medical insurance system, which was praised as a "remarkable achievement" by the World Health Organization (WHO).

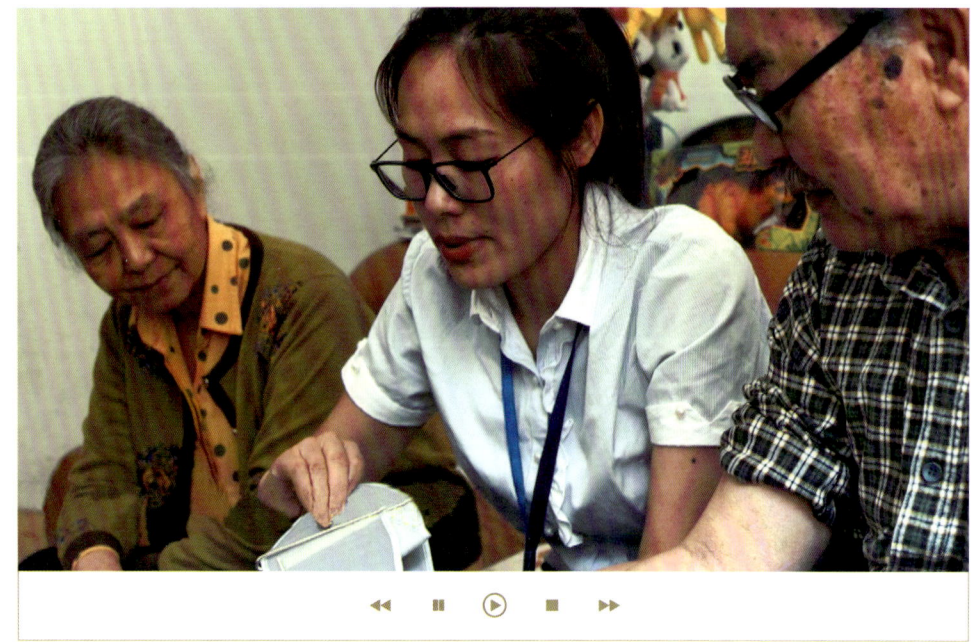

鼓浪屿医院健康管理师杨燕入户看望蔡宝瑞老两口
Yang Yan, a health management worker at the Gulangyu Hospital, visits Cai Baorui and her husband.

家庭医生

中国的家庭医生非贵族专属。它是这个拥有十三亿多人口的大国，要让人人享有更高等级公共医疗服务的决心和承诺。

为优化配置医疗卫生资源，福建省厦门市探索建立分级诊疗制度，从大医院门诊占比高的慢性病入手，"两病"（糖尿病、高血压病）探路，创设"三师共管"团队服务模式。"三师共管"是指由医院专科医师、基层家庭医师和健康管理师共同组成的医疗团队服务模式，即由一位全科医生、一位健康管理师和大医院的专科医师组成团队，共同服务居民。在厦门市三十八家公立基层医疗卫生机构中，厦门大学附属第一医院鼓浪屿医院在2016年年度考评中名列第一。

鼓浪屿医院健康管理师杨燕的名片上写着："5+2，白+黑，全天候呵护您的健康。"这天，杨燕来到居民蔡宝瑞家中。蔡宝瑞的老伴儿在元旦前一天尿血，痛不欲生。幸好马上可以联系到杨燕。

蔡宝瑞说："我经常讲，（简直）比自己的女儿还要亲。我们心里很踏实，不怕。乐呵乐呵，三百六十五天，我们都是高高兴兴地过。而且现在共产党对我们老年人更关心。我们这是生活在太平盛世里，你不（是）说我们要多活几年（吗），肯定的，是不是？"

杨燕说，我们就是居民和全科医生的一个桥梁，一个沟通（媒介）。所以我们平时这一块入户的工作，与居民交流的工作是做得非常细致的，会经常入户。

中国的目标，是力争到2020年基本实现家庭医生签约服务制度全覆盖，让百姓都有自己的家庭医生。这是写进《"健康中国2030"规划纲要》的全世界最大的健康工程。中国织就了全世界最大的基本医疗保障网，被世界卫生组织称赞为举世瞩目的成就。

❀ 更多年轻人关注老年人的生活、健康
More young people now pay attention to the health conditions of their old parents to ensure they lead a high-quality life during their twilight years

❀ 鼓浪屿医院健康管理师杨燕与蔡宝瑞老两口一起散步
Yang Yan, a health management worker at the Gulangyu Hospital in Xiamen, Fujian Province, takes a walk with Cai Baorui and her husband.

❀ 鼓浪屿医院两位健康管理师在路上商议工作
Two health management workers from the Gulangyu Hospital exchange views on their work on the road.

THE ELDERLY WILL BE LOOKED AFTER PROPERLY

China is moving faster towards an aged society. Over the past five years, the government has invested 5 billion yuan to build 100,000 nursing homes in rural areas and 110,000 community-level elder service centers.

Niu Yanxing and his wife come from Shandong Province. They have been staying in Sunshine Senior Service Center located in Tangyuan village, Fenshui Town, Tonglu County, Hangzhou City, Zhejiang Province for a month to receive medical care. The senior couple plans to stay for the rest of their lives here.

By the end of 2017, social security card holders had been allowed to handle medical cost settlement between different cities around China. The card enables them to enjoy 102 items of welfare.

As the world's only country with an elderly population of more than 200 million, China has elevated pensions for 12 consecutive years. The average life span of Chinese people has increased to 76 years, five years higher than the world average.

Behind this miracle is China's commitment to building a moderately prosperous society in all respects that benefits all.

浙江省杭州市桐庐县
Tonglu County in Hangzhou, Zhejiang Province.

桐庐县分水镇塘园村阳光养老服务中心的工作人员为牛衍兴老两口量血压
A worker at the Sunshine Senior Service Center in Tangyuan Village of Fenshui Town, Tonglu County, measures blood pressure for Niu Yanxing and his wife.

塘园村阳光养老服务中心主任汪亚君问老人，饭菜对胃口吗
Wang Yajun, director of the Sunshine Senior Service Center in Tangyuan Village, asked seniors if the meal tastes good.

老有所养

扫码看本节短视频
Scan to watch the short video

老龄化，正在加速向中国而来。这五年，国家累计投入五十亿元。十万个农村幸福院、十一万个社区居家养老服务中心，已经建立起来。

牛衍兴两口子从山东来，已经在浙江省杭州市桐庐县分水镇塘园村的阳光养老服务中心调理了一个月，老两口打算就在这儿养老了。

到2017年底，全国的社保卡基本实现异地结算，一百零二项福利用一张卡就能办妥。

作为世界上唯一一个老年人口超过两亿的国家，中国做到了养老金连续十二年上调。中国人的平均寿命已经提高到七十六岁，比世界平均水平超出五岁。

生命奇迹的背后，是中国对小康建设的全面覆盖。

塘源村阳光养老服务中心外貌
A panoramic view of the Sunshine Senior Service Center.

牛衍兴老两口在院内散步
Niu Yanxing and his wife take a walk in the courtyard of the senior service center.

牛衍兴老两口在用餐
Niu Yanxing and his wife having dinner.

SECURITY ASSURANCE

Public security is an "invisible guard" for achieving the goal of building a moderately prosperous society in all respects. Every time a crisis approaches, the nation offers a strong shoulder for the people to rely on.

What makes people feel really safe is the Chinese People's Liberation Army. On July 30, 2017, President Xi Jinping delivered a speech at a military parade celebrating the 90th anniversary of the founding of the PLA, in which he said: "I believe that our heroic army has the confidence and capacity to defeat all invading enemies and safeguard national sovereignty, security and development interests."

火箭军在戈壁训练场组织实战化训练，进行实弹发射
The PLA Rocket Force conducts a live-fire drill in the desert training ground.

空军猛士
A Chinese Air Force pilot.

直升机演习
A helicopter in military training.

直升机起降训练
Helicopters taking off and landing.

安全保障

扫码看本节短视频
Scan to watch the short video

公共安全,保障小康的隐形卫士。任何时候危机来临,总有坚强的臂膀让人民依靠。

让人民真正有安全感的还有这支威武之师——人民军队。2017年7月30日,习近平主席在庆祝中国人民解放军建军90周年阅兵式上说道:"我坚信,我们的英雄军队有信心、有能力打败一切来犯之敌!我们的英雄军队有信心、有能力维护国家主权、安全、发展利益!"

2016年12月26日,中国海军航母编队在远海大洋乘风破浪
December 26, 2016: The aircraft carrier fleet of the Chinese Navy on voyage.

坚强守护卫士——装甲部队接受检阅
Armored troops in a military parade.

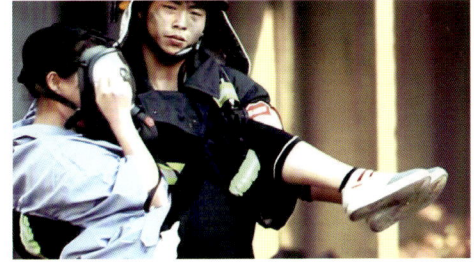

消防救援
Fire rescue.

警察巡逻
Police officers in patrol.

2019年10月1日，庆祝中华人民共和国成立70周年大会在北京天安门广场隆重举行。图为阅兵仪式后的群众游行

October 1, 2019: A military parade in honor of the 70th anniversary of the founding of the People's Republic of China is held at Tian'anmen Square in Beijing. Pictured is a mass pageant after the military parade.

扫码看同内容电影
Scan to watch the film

扫码看同类专题片
Scan to watch similar documentaries

第六章

▶ 开放中国
VI A MORE OPEN CHINA

坚强守护来自于强盛的国力，中国深知正是过去四十年的改革开放成就了今日中国位于世界前列的国际地位。中国也深信唯有开放，才能与世界一道持续繁荣。

National strength is a prerequisite for a country's security and stability. The Chinese people are aware that the past 40 years of reform and opening up lifted China to its status as a world-leading economy and believe that only further opening up can enable China to achieve enduring prosperity along with the rest of the world.

THE EVACUATION OF OVERSEAS CHINESE IN YEMEN

Wherever you are on the planet, the motherland is always solid backing. The Chinese government always takes immediate action to rescue its citizens in trouble.

One feels warm when he is brought back to the motherland.

One feels proud as a Chinese citizen.

One feels lucky as a Chinese citizen.

One gains a sense of security as a Chinese citizen.

On March 26, 2015, the international forces joined by Saudi Arabia, Egypt, Jordan, Sudan and other Gulf countries launched a military operation against Hussein's armed forces in Yemen. The situation on the ground suddenly became tense. Experienced the evacuation of overseas Chinese in Yemen, Zhang Zuohe from the China State Construction Engineering Corporation (CSCEC) said: "The corporation's two subsidiaries in Yemen were robbed in March 2015."

Zeng Bo from the CSCEC recalled that during Yemen's civil war, the glass windows of their office building were broken by stray bullets.

At the scene of the evacuation, Tian Qi, Chinese ambassador extraordinary and plenipotentiary to Yemen, said through the loudspeaker: "The security situation was deteriorating in Yemen. The CPC Central Committee, the State Council and the Central Military Commission care deeply about the safety of all Chinese citizens in the country. Today, we launch an emergency evacuation from Yemen."

"As the ship approached, a voice said, 'Chinese compatriots, this is the PLA Navy. The Central Military Commission sent us to escort you home.' All Chinese citizens waiting at the port shouted: 'Long Live the Motherland!' At that moment, every one of us felt safe and a sense of the greatness of China," recalled Zhang Zuohe from the CSCEC.

中国军舰赶往也门参与撤侨
Chinese naval ships on their way to war-ridden Yemen to evacuate Chinese nationals.

中国同胞在岸上向军舰挥舞国旗
Chinese nationals wave national flags towards the Chinese naval ships that came to take them home.

中国军舰接同胞回家
A Chinese naval ship escorting overseas Chinese back home.

也门撤侨

无论你身在何处,祖国都是你的坚强后盾。

有一种速度,叫中国救援;

有一种感动,叫祖国带我回家;

有一种骄傲,叫我是中国人;

有一种幸运,叫我是中国人;

有一种安全感,叫我是中国人。

2015年3月26日,由沙特阿拉伯和埃及、约旦、苏丹等其他海湾国家参加的国际联军在也门发动打击胡赛武装的军事行动,当地局势骤然紧张。

经历了也门撤侨的中国建筑股份有限公司工作人员张作合在事后接受采访时说:"机关和两个公司同时遭到抢劫。"

中国建筑股份有限公司曾波对记者说,当时打仗,子弹都穿过了我们办公楼的玻璃。

中华人民共和国驻也门共和国特命全权大使田琦在撤侨现场通过扩音器讲话说:"当前,也门安全局势恶化。党中央、国务院、中央军委高度重视,十分关心大家的生命安危,我们今天特别安排,紧急撤离也门。"

张作合说:"看着船慢慢靠近,开始喊话:'中国同胞们,我们是中国人民解放军海军,中央军委下令让我们保护你们回家。'大家就在那儿喊:'祖国万岁!'那时觉得心里很踏实,感觉中国很伟大。"

中国驻也门大使田琦在也门撤侨现场
Tian Qi, Chinese ambassador to Yemen, at the site of evacuation.

中国驻阿曼大使于福龙与登舰同胞握手
Yu Fulong, Chinese ambassador to Oman, shakes hands with an evacuated Chinese national aboard the ship.

CHINA-EUROPE FREIGHT TRAINS

In autumn 2013, China introduced the Belt and Road Initiative. Thanks to joint efforts from all countries along the routes, the economic connection between China and Europe is becoming closer and stronger.

On March 29, 2014, a fully-loaded train from China's Chongqing arrived at the port of Duisburg, Germany, during Chinese President Xi Jinping's visit to the port.

The launch of China-Europe freight train service marked the highest density of train traffic shuttling across the Eurasian Continent since the birth of rails. So far, a total of 430,000 TEUs of cargo have been transported along the routes.

杜伊斯堡港
The port of Duisburg.

第 141 列厦门—莫斯科中欧班列
The 141st CRE Xiamen-Moscow freight train.

成都—波兰罗兹中欧班列
The CRE Chengdu-Lodz freight train.

中欧班列

扫码看本节短视频
Scan to watch the short video

2013 年秋，中国提出了"一带一路"倡议，在沿线国家共同努力下，中欧经济的联系更加紧密。

2014 年 3 月 29 日，中国国家主席习近平来到德国杜伊斯堡港，三声锣响后，一列从中国重庆始发的列车满载货物，缓缓驶入。

中欧班列，实现了自铁路诞生以来，第一次如此高密度地在亚欧大陆横贯穿行，往来运送货物已达四十三万标箱。

行驶中的中欧班列
A CRE freight train in operation.

缓缓驶达目的地的中欧班列
A CRE freight train reaching its destination.

成都—波兰罗兹中欧班列
The CRE Chengdu-Lodz freight train.

繁忙的集装箱中心站
A busy container yard.

THE BELT AND ROAD INITIATIVE

Thanks to implementation of the Belt and Road Initiative, China has shared its development experience with Africa, enabling the continent to move towards prosperity.

Every project under the Belt and Road Initiative has been implemented with the principles of extensive consultation, joint contributions and shared benefits. The goal of China's opening up is to benefit not only its own people but also people of countries on the Belt and Road.

The supervisor of the No. 1 workshop of the Guangzhou Huajian factory in Ethiopia, who was named Guang Zhou in Chinese, and his colleagues.

Zhang Huarong, chairman of Huajian Group, talks with employees.

More than 4,000 local young people hired in the Eastern Industry Zone in Ethiopia.

Zhang Huarong, board chairman of the Huajian Group in Guangzhou, Guangdong Province, said that local employees in Ethiopia like and respect him. "This is because they recognize China's inclusive and shared development concept and economic development model."

These Ethiopian young employees have learned technology and management from China. Zhang Huarong gave each of them a Chinese name. Young Ethiopian men like these hope their hometowns can become as developed and prosperous as Chinese metropolises.

A 25-year-old Ethiopian employee, whose Chinese name is Guang Zhou, has been appointed supervisor of the No. 1 workshop of the Huajian's factory in Ethiopia. He remarked: "Zhang Huarong likes us, and we like him too."

Within just two years, Ethiopian employees' shoemaking skills have reached the world medium-high standard. Chinese companies are not only bringing new technologies, but also helping Ethiopia form a complete leather industrial chain.

The Huajian factory in Ethiopia is equipped with nine modern production lines identical to its factory in China.

Guang Zhou is happy to work in such a factory.

In the Huajian factory in Ethiopia, a manager like Guang Zhou can earn a monthly salary equivalent to 5,000 yuan, and even an ordinary worker can earn income twice the local average.

"I now oversee more than 1,400 Ethiopian employees," said Guang Zhou, "Truly, I am quite happy now."

China has built 56 industrial parks and economic and trade cooperation zones in more than 20 countries along the Belt and Road. Over the past five years, they have created 180,000 jobs in those countries.

On May 14, 2017, the First Belt and Road Forum for International Cooperation opened in Beijing. In his speech at the forum, Chinese President Xi Jinping

"一带一路"倡议

扫码看本节短视频
Scan to watch the short video

"一带一路"建设正在把中国的发展经验传递给非洲，带动非洲繁荣。

翻开"一带一路"的工程图谱，每一个都是这样共商，共建，共享。既要让自己过得好，也要让别人过得好，这是中国对外开放的追求。

华坚集团董事长张华荣在埃塞俄比亚的工厂
Zhang Huarong, chairman of Huajian Group, visits the corporation's factory in Ethiopia.

这里是埃塞俄比亚的东方工业园，有四千多个当地年轻人在这里上班。

广州华坚集团董事长张华荣说，他们非常喜欢我，其实对中国这种包容共享的发展理念和经济发展的模式，在他们心里有深深的认同感。

这几位小伙子，都到中国学习过技术和管理。张华荣给他们起了中文名字，小伙子们也希望自己的家乡能像中国的大都市一样富强。

这位中文名叫"广州"的小伙子刚满二十五岁，就已经是华坚埃塞俄比亚工厂第一车间的主管了。他评价张华荣说："他很喜欢我们，我们也很喜欢他。"

短短两年，埃塞俄比亚员工的制鞋技术已经达到全球中等水平。中国企业带来的新技术使埃塞俄比亚有了完整的皮革产业链。

厂里九条现代化生产线都和中国国内的生产线一模一样。

能在这样的工厂工作，"广州"觉得很幸福。

华坚集团埃塞俄比亚工厂第一车间主管"广州"在与工厂员工交流
The supervisor of the No. 1 workshop of the Guangzhou Huajian factory in Ethiopia, who was named Guang Zhou in Chinese, talks with his colleagues.

埃塞俄比亚的东方工业园
The Eastern Industry Zone in Ethiopia.

华坚集团埃塞俄比亚工厂员工
Employees at Huajian Group's factory in Ethiopia.

华坚集团埃塞俄比亚工厂生产车间内员工在工作
A worker at a workshop of Huajian Group's factory in Ethiopia.

said: "A Chinese saying goes, 'Peaches and plums do not speak, but they are so attractive that a path is formed below the trees'… In pursuing the Belt and Road Initiative, we should focus on the fundamental issue of development, release the growth potential of various countries and achieve economic integration and interconnected development that delivers benefits to all."

在华坚，像"广州"这样的管理人员每月薪水相当于五千元人民币，即便是普通员工，收入也是当地平均工资的两倍。

"广州"说，我现在管差不多一千四百多个埃塞俄比亚员工，所以我现在说实话非常开心，很开心。

像这样的工业园和经贸合作区，中国在"一带一路"沿线二十多个国家，已经建设了五十六个，五年来创造了就业岗位十八万个。

在 2017 年 5 月 14 日，"一带一路"国际合作高峰论坛上，习近平主席说，"桃李不言，下自成蹊"……推进"一带一路"建设，要聚焦发展这个根本性问题，释放各国发展潜力，实现经济大融合、发展大联动、成果大共享。

华坚集团埃塞俄比亚工厂内众多员工正在工作
Workers at Huajian Group's factory in Ethiopia.

"广州"在与同事交流
Guang Zhou is communicating with his colleague.

华坚集团埃塞俄比亚工厂生产车间员工们在认真工作
Workers at Huajian Group's factory in Ethiopia.

中国力量 THE CHINESE STRENGTH

❀ 越南龙江工业园一瞥
The Longjiang Industrial Park in Vietnam.

❀ 中埃苏伊士经贸合作区
The China-Egypt TEDA Suez Economic and Trade Cooperation Zone.

❀ 中白工业园
The China-Belarus Industrial Park.

❁ 泰中罗勇工业园
Thai-Chinese Rayong Industrial Zone.

❁ 中柬西哈努克经济特区
Sihanoukville Special Economic Zone, a China-Cambodia joint venture.

❁ 与世界一道持续繁荣
China is willing to achieve common prosperity with other countries in the world.

CHINA'S VOICE AT INTERNATIONAL CONFERENCES

China will keep its door open and will open the door wider.

China has shared feasible advice for promoting regional economic integration.

China has offered wisdom and solutions to promote reform of the global governance system.

...

Never before has China been as close to the center of the world stage and realization of the dream of national rejuvenation as it is today

At the 2015 UN Conference on Climate Change in Paris.

At the 22nd APEC Economic Leaders' Meeting on November 11, 2014, Chinese President Xi Jinping said in his speech that construction of an interconnectivity platform and the development of APEC depend on efforts from all parties concerned.

China has made commitments to actively address global climate change.

At the UN climate change conference in Paris on November 30, 2015, Chinese President Xi Jinping said in his speech that China has always been an active player in tackling climate change globally.

The AIIB (Asian Infrastructure Investment Bank), a multilateral financial institution proposed by Chinese President Xi Jinping, was officially established on December 25, 2015. At the opening ceremony of AIIB on January 16, 2016, Chinese President Xi Jinping said that all international financial institutions including the AIIB are welcome to join in implementation of the Belt and Road Initiative.

China has offered wisdom and solutions to promote reform of the global governance system.

At the Hangzhou G20 Summit on September

国际会议上的中国声音

开放的大门将越开越大。

推动区域经济一体化，中国提出可行的建议。

推动全球治理体系变革，中国提出智慧的方案。

…………

今日中国，前所未有地走近世界舞台中央，前所未有地接近实现中华民族伟大复兴的梦想。

❀ 2016年二十国集团领导人杭州峰会晚会地点——杭州曲院风荷公园
Quyuan Fenghe Park, the venue for the evening gala of the 2016 G20 Summit in Hangzhou.

在2014年11月11日，亚太经合组织第二十二次领导人非正式会议上，习近平主席说，推进互联互通的联接平台，亚太经合组织的发展壮大有赖于大家共同支持。

应对全球气候变化，中国做出积极的承诺。

在2015年11月30日，气候变化巴黎大会上，习近平主席说，中国一直是全球应对气候变化事业的积极参与者。

2015年12月25日，由习近平主席提出筹建倡议的亚洲基础设施投资银行正式成立。在2016年1月16日，亚洲基础设施投资银行开业仪式上，习近平主席说，我们将继续欢迎，包括亚投行在内的新老国际金融机构，共同参与"一带一路"建设。

推动全球治理体系变革，中国提出智慧的方案。

2016年9月4日，二十国集团领导人杭州峰会上，习近平主席说，为世界经济开出一剂标本兼治、综合施策的药方。

自由"逆全球化"思潮，中国发出响亮的声音。

在2017年1月17日，达沃斯世界经济论坛2017年年会上，习近平主席说，中国将大力建设共同发展的对外开放格局。

中国的大门对世界始终是打开的，不会关上。开着门，世界能够进入中国，中国也才能走向世界。

2017年9月4日，金砖国家领导人厦门会晤时，习近平主席说，我们应该推动建设开放型世界经济，使之惠及各国人民。

今日中国，前所未有地走近世界舞台中央，前所未有地接近实现中华民族伟大复兴的梦想。

在2017年1月17日，达沃斯世界经济论坛2017年年会上，习近平主席说，历史是勇敢者创造的，让我们拿出信心，采取行动，携手向着未来前进！

4, 2016, Chinese President Xi Jinping introduced remedies for the sluggish world economy to embark on a road of robust, sustainable, balanced and inclusive growth.

China is providing a loud voice against the anti-globalization mentality.

At the annual meeting of the World Economic Forum in Davos on January 17, 2017, Chinese President Xi Jinping vowed that China would pursue common development through further opening up.

China will keep its door wide open, which is the only way China and the world can approach each other.

At the BRICS summit in Xiamen on September 4, 2017, Chinese President Xi Jinping called for an open and inclusive world economy that benefits people of all countries.

Never before has China been as close to the center of the world stage and realization of the dream of national rejuvenation as it is today.

On January 17, 2017, Chinese President Xi Jinping said at the annual meeting of the World Economic Forum in Davos: "History is created by the brave. Let us boost confidence, take actions and march arm-in-arm toward a bright future."

The opening ceremony of the Asian Infrastructure Investment Bank in 2016.

At the 2017 annual conference of the World Economic Forum in Davos, Switzerland.

✿ 2017年金砖国家领导人厦门会晤的一个场景
At the 2017 BRICS Summit in Xiamen, Fujian Province.

✿ 2017年"一带一路"国际合作高峰论坛
At the Belt and Road Forum for International Cooperation in 2017.

扫码看同内容电影
Scan to watch the film

第七章

▶ 共筑中国梦
VII BUILD THE CHINESE DREAM TOGETHER

  2017 年 10 月 18 日，习近平总书记在中国共产党第十九次全国代表大会作报告时说："同志们！使命呼唤担当，使命引领未来。我们要不负人民重托，无愧历史选择，在新时代中国特色社会主义的伟大实践中，以党的坚强领导和顽强奋斗，激励全体中华儿女不断奋进，凝聚起同心共筑中国梦的磅礴力量！"

  2017 年 10 月 25 日，习近平总书记在十九届中央政治局常委同中外记者见面会上说："人民对美好生活的向往，就是我们的奋斗目标。"

  On October 18, 2017, General Secretary and Chinese President Xi Jinping said at the 19th CPC National Congress: "Our mission is a call to action; our mission steers the course to the future. We must live up to the trust the people have placed in us and prove ourselves worthy of history's choice. In the great endeavors of building socialism with Chinese characteristics in the new era, let us get behind the strong leadership of the Party and engage in a tenacious struggle. Let all of us, the sons and daughters of the Chinese nation, come together, keep going, and create a mighty force that enables us to realize the Chinese Dream."

  On October 25, 2017, while leading newly elected members of the Standing Committee of the 19th CPC Central Committee Political Bureau to meet the press, General Secretary Xi Jinping noted: "Our goal must be to meet the people's aspirations to live a better life."

中国力量 THE CHINESE STRENGTH

BEAUTIFUL LANDSCAPES

In the wind and rain, the voyage is magnificent; thousands of miles, the sunshine is in my heart.

My dream shines ahead, and your faith lights courage. We struggle to move forward by the way of relay. Let's sow hope and cultivate the land. We are confident that we can move forward and see the Chinese people go to a new world.

向未来挺进
Marching towards the future.

大地绿意盎然
Lush vegetation.

田野风光更加迷人
A vast expanse of farmland.

大美山河

扫码看本节短视频
Scan to watch the short video

风里雨里，航程壮丽，千里万里，阳光在心里。

我的梦想照耀前方，你的信仰点燃勇气。我们一起奋进接力，让我们一起播种希望，耕耘土地。我们自信，我们前行，看中华儿女走向新的天地。

◎ 孕育了中华儿女的黄河依旧波澜壮阔
The Yellow River, known as the "mother river of the Chinese nation," remains torrential and magnificent.

曲折回环的长城见证着中国的发展变迁
The zigzagging Great Wall has witnessed the development of China over thousands of years.

中国力量 THE CHINESE STRENGTH

祖国大美风光（组图）
Beautiful landscapes of China.

PROSPEROUS CITIES

◎ 城市建设日新月异
China has seen increasing urbanization.

城市更加繁荣

扫码看本节短视频
Scan to watch the short video

◈ 地处京津冀发展圈，天津市经济和社会蓬勃发展
The city of Tianjin, located in the Beijing-Tianjin-Hebei economic circle, is witnessing rapid development.

◈ 位于长江三角洲城市群中心的上海一片繁荣景象
The bustling Shanghai, the center of the Yangtze River Delta city cluster.

◈ 位于海南经济特区内秀美的三亚风光
The city of Sanya, located in Hainan Special Economic Zone, is noted for its picturesque landscape.

古老与现代交相辉映的北京城市风光
The cityscape of Beijing combines tradition and modernity.

VIGOROUS DEVELOPMENT IN ALL ASPECTS OF SOCIETY

中国体育健儿为国家争光添彩,中国女排多次在世界级比赛上勇夺冠军
Chinese athletes have won honors for their motherland on the international arena. The Chinese Women's Volleyball Team has won champions at many world competitions.

社会事业兴旺发达
China's social undertakings have become more thriving.

社会事业蓬勃发展

扫码看本节短视频
Scan to watch the short video

❀ 基础设施建设更加全面
China's infrastructure construction has entered a new level.

❀ 海洋开发与保护并重（组图）
China places equal emphasis on exploration and protection of marine resources.

中国力量 THE CHINESE STRENGTH

MILITARY DEVELOPMENT AND NATIONAL SECURITY

◎ 中国海军新型潜艇
A new-type submarine of the Chinese Navy.

国防和军队建设

扫码看本节短视频
Scan to watch the short video

❀ 中国空军加强远海训练
The Chinese Air Force strengthens ocean-going training to enhance its strategic abilities.

❀ 中国陆军坦克部队随时备战
Tanks of the Chinese Army.

❀ 空军飞行员驾驶着新型战斗机在蓝天巡视领空
A pilot of the Chinese Air Force drives an advanced fighter to patrol China's territorial airspace.

"辽宁号"航空母舰,是中国人民解放军海军第一艘可以搭载固定翼飞机的航空母舰
The Liaoning is the first aircraft carrier that can deploy fixed-wing planes commissioned into the Chinese People's Liberation Army Navy.

中国海军"辽宁号"航母编队演练
The Liaoning aircraft carrier fleet of the Chinese Navy in drill.

FULLY OPENING UP

❂ 中国与世界同繁荣，同发展
China works with other countries in the world to promote shared prosperity and common development.

❂ 中国的大门始终开放，与世界各国共同发展（组图）
China has always opened its door to the world and is willing to realize common development with all other countries.

全面对外开放

扫码看本节短视频
Scan to watch the short video

◉ 促进各行各业与国际社会的交流与合作
China has strengthened exchange and cooperation with the international community across the board.

◉ 中外友谊更加紧密（组图）
The friendship between China and other countries continues growing.

ALL ETHNIC GROUPS UNITE TO REALIZE THE CHINESE DREAM

❀ 中国青年一代充满活力
Chinese youth are full of vigor and vitality.

❀ 人民群众安居乐业（组图）
The Chinese people now lead a better-off life.

民族团结,共同实现中国梦

扫码看本节短视频
Scan to watch the short video

❀ 用歌舞表达对祖国的祝福
Greeting the motherland through songs and dances.

❀ 文艺活动丰富多彩(组图)
Colorful cultural and artistic activities.

中国力量 THE CHINESE STRENGTH

各民族团结一心，共同发展
All ethnic groups in China unite together to seek common prosperity.

杭州西湖雷峰塔美丽风光
The beautiful scenery of West Lake in Hangzhou.

中国未来更加辉煌
China will be more glorious in the future.

POSTSCRIPT

This photo book is based on the documentary film *Amazing China*, which showcases the remarkable achievements of China's reform and development since the 18th CPC National Congress and embodies the great practice of Xi Jinping Thought on Socialism with Chinese Characteristics for a New Era. With impressive visual effect and beautiful images, this documentary film demonstrates the glamour and charm of China as a major country from various perspectives through recording the breathtaking videos of several marvelous megaprojects conducted by China and stories behind them and unveiling the "Chinese spirit" embedded in those "Chinese miracles". Authorized by the copyright holder of this documentary film, China Pictorial Press adapted the script and images of the film and published the photo book in Chinese-English (bilingual edition), French, Spanish, Arabic, etc.

In the process of adaptation, our staff made a re-creation based on the documentary film's content while giving full play to the advantage of online videos, achieving online-offline interaction and combining paper book with online videos. The photo book provides three forms of video watching with QR codes: ① Scan to watch the film; ② Scan to watch the TV documentary series *Glorious China*; ③ Scan to watch the short video of each episode.

The successful publication of this photo book is attributed to joint efforts of many individuals and institutions. Hereby, we would like to extend our sincere gratitude to China Media Group and China Film Co., Ltd. for their authorization and service, to leaders of China International Publishing Group (also known as China Foreign Languages Publishing Administration) for their strong support, to leaders and staffers of China.org.cn (also known as China Internet Information Center) for their platform and technological support. Meanwhile, we would also like to thank all of the staff who made contributions to the adaptation, compilation, translation, photo supply and selection, book design, publication, video editing, webpage design and other work for this book.

We sincerely hope that as a fruit of joint efforts of our team, this book will win popularity among readers.

China Pictorial Press
November 2019

后记

本画册取材于纪录片《厉害了，我的国》。该片反映了党的十八大以来中国改革和发展的卓越成就，反映了习近平新时代中国特色社会主义思想的伟大实践，影片以超震撼的视觉，精美的画面，多角度展现了我国的大国风采，记录了多个超级工程的震撼影像以及背后的故事，挖掘了"中国奇迹"背后的"中国精神"。根据电影版权方的授权，我社对电影文字和画面进行了改编，将先后出版中英对照、法文、西文、阿文等文版的画册作品。

改编过程中，画册工作人员根据纪录片的内容脉络进行了再创作，充分发挥了互联网视频优势，体现了线上线下互动、纸质阅读与视频观看相结合的特点。画册中共添加了三种二维码：①扫码看电影，②扫码看《辉煌中国》电视专题片，③扫码看每节专题或故事单元的短视频。

本画册的出版，得益于多个单位的配合，凝结着很多人的心血。感谢电影版权方中国中央广播电视总台、中国电影集团股份有限公司的授权和服务！感谢中国国际出版集团（中国外文局）领导的大力支持！感谢中国网（中国国际互联网新闻中心）领导及同事们的平台援助和技术支持！同时，也感谢改编、编辑、翻译、选图、供图、装帧设计、出版、视频剪辑、网页制作等各方面工作人员付出的辛勤劳动！

衷心希望团队共同努力的成果，能够赢得读者的喜爱！

中国画报出版社
2019 年 11 月

画册出品：中国外文出版发行事业局
Presented by China International Publishing Group
版权授权：中国电影股份有限公司
Authorized by China Film Co., Ltd.